A PERSON-MINDED MINISTRY

A PERSON-MINDED MINISTRY

By

RICHARD HENRY EDWARDS

COKESBURY PRESS
NASHVILLE

SET UP, ELECTROTYPED, PRINTED, AND BOUND
BY THE PARTHENON PRESS AT NASHVILLE,
TENNESSEE, UNITED STATES OF AMERICA

Yours for person - middleness
& Creative relations

Richard Henry Edwards

This book is dedicated

to

EVERY ONE OF THE SOUTHERN MINISTERS

who shared in the searches out of which it has grown

especially to

WILLIAM M. ALEXANDER

true friend, wise counselor, courageous administrator

and to

ALVA W. TAYLOR

truth-teller, fighter for social justice, friend of
mountain children

FOREWORD

THIS book grew in topsoil; but, like alfalfa, it has deep roots in subsoil. It sprouted by reason of gracious invitations to "Ministers' Weeks" at Emory University, at Atlanta, Georgia; Southern Methodist University, at Dallas, Texas; and Bethel College, McKenzie, Tennessee, all early in 1937. It hibernated under the winter snows of upstate New York in 1938 but broke loose again in the spring of 1939 in summer schools of Southern Methodist ministers at Conway, Arkansas; Emory, Virginia; and Lynchburg, Virginia, all in June of 1939. That's topsoil—mellow, warm, and hospitable—soil that would quicken any sterile Yankee to yield whatever he had in him.

Subsoil is more difficult to describe—buried out of sight in the past. Some deep roots are traceable, however: discussions with other ministers and would-be ministers in courses, interviews, and conferences at the University of Chicago; at Colgate-Rochester and Auburn Seminaries; in New York at Union Seminary; at Lake Junaluska, North Carolina; in Nashville, Tennessee, at Scarritt College; and here at Happy Valley. Besides these, there have been some years of striving to be a minister myself. A sort of mysterious distillate has seeped down into the subsoil out of all these. The habit of cocking a critical eye at visiting preachers through the years at Yale, Wisconsin, and Cornell put into the soil a bit of lime, which has, I hope, not wholly lost its savor but rather sweetened both top and subsoil, out of which has grown this hay or flower. As I give it back to those who nourished it, I pray that, like the roots of alfalfa, it may carry fertilizing nodules to enrich the soils in which it grew.

This book is intended for ministers in the most inclusive

sense—ordained and unordained. Having, as a Congregational minister, scant respect for the doctrine of the clergy as a separate order from the laity, but believing profoundly in the priesthood of all believers, I mean this book for all sorts and kinds of ministers who would heighten their skills in dealing with other persons, who love the person-mindedness of Jesus, and who find Him the superlative artist in creative relationships both human and divine. It is high time for ordained ministers to rethink their own presuppositions, methods, and functions in relation to modern persons. Many of the unordained are outstripping us in the quality and magnitude of their human sharing—and this often without conscious use of the incalculable resources for human therapy that are in Jesus. Many ordained ministers are bewildered between the old and new as to emphasis, method, and function. Emphases out of balance are being widely urged upon ministers as if each were the whole instead of an aspect, as, for example, social action, mental hygiene, preaching, or parish organization —all indispensable in their proper places, but each rightly to be seen as an aspect, not the whole.

This book represents a number of group searches for true balance among emphases, processes, and functions in the ministry. In the light of a considerable sampling of the actual experiences of ministers who are wrestling with the problems of modern persons, we recognize the wide variety of services being rendered and seek a unifying theme in an emphasis upon creative relationships.

Unordained ministers, such as are many doctors, nurses, Christian Association secretaries, Red Cross and social workers, schoolteachers, parents, and consulting psychologists, have discovered techniques and developed skills of which thousands of us ordained ministers are ignorant. This book is a suggestion of cross-fertilization between the two groups as well as an orientation study for ordained ministers.

Grateful acknowledgment is made to the International Council of Religious Education for permission to quote selections from the American Standard Edition of the Revised Bible; to the University of Chicago Press for permission to quote selections from *The Bible, an American Translation,* by J. M. P. Smith and Edgar J. Goodspeed; and to other authors and publishers who have kindly granted permission to quote copyrighted material.

Grateful acknowledgment is also made to the following friends who have read all or parts of the manuscript and made valued suggestions: Dr. William M. Alexander, Secretary, Department of Schools and Colleges, General Board of Christian Education, Methodist Episcopal Church, South; Mrs. Carolyn Curtis Brown of London, England, and Lisle, New York; Mrs. Martin D. Hardin of Ithaca, New York; Reverend Hugh Anderson Moran, Presbyterian University Pastor at Cornell University; and Mrs. Herbert K. Twitchell of Setauket, New York. My thanks are also due to Mrs. Elrita Crawford of Nashville, Tennessee, for assistance with the final manuscript. I am indebted above all to my wife, Anna Camp Edwards, whose wisdom and constant encouragement have brought me light and leading.

RICHARD HENRY EDWARDS

Happy Valley,
Lisle, New York.

CONTENTS

Chapter Four

Chapter Five

FOUR FUNCTIONS OF A PERSON-MINDED MINISTER

Chapter Six

Chapter Seven

I

PERSON-MINDEDNESS

THE word person-mindedness began to be meaningful to me in the winter of 1933 while conducting a course on pastoral counseling with ministers at Colgate-Rochester. The word has changed my mind since then. Even last night I lay awake a long time seeing new lights hidden away in it. It seemed as if I were a boy again, floating in my boat on the old Tioughnioga, leaning over the boat's edge, looking down into clear depths of beauty where brilliant little sunfish glided in and out amid the roots of old stumps under the shore. They were like flashes of insight, lighting up tangled old obscurities. They keep on gliding in and out.

"What a word!" one of the ministers had said. "It's worth taking the course to get it." At the moment I didn't suppose he meant the rest of the course was so dull that this word was the one bright spot in it. But maybe he did. You never can tell all that ministers mean by what they say. Some of us tend to think that saying things is our whole business. Anyway, the word got him as it has me, and it may come to suggest fresh lights on life to those who follow through these meditations. We can do little more than make a beginning together —catch glimpses here and there. Yet those who keep on looking sharply down into its hidden depths will continue to find in it living values. It becomes indeed the clue to an interpretation of life and a way of life that are like nothing

15

else so much as a river filled with gleaming things, flowing in sunlight and moving toward the sea.

Persons are to have our attention. They need to be freshly seen—all sorts and kinds of persons at all stages of growth: these strange two-legged creatures, erect for action or supine for sleep, clad in native hair and furs or in cut-aways or pajamas, climbing anciently out of danger into trees or modernly into danger in airplanes; creatures with beautiful supple bodies, with muscles, nerves, mysterious glands, and each with three or four quarts of miracle-working blood apiece—with eyes and ears and noses, with tongues for taste and talk, with brains and hearts, with viscera and organs of sex, with arms and legs and fingers and toes, all hung on a limber mechanical framework and covered with smooth elastic integument. They are all animals with habits and individual histories. They are more than animals. They have personal awareness as to who, what, and where they are. They are *persons,* with atttitudes, prejudices, hopes and fears, hates and loves, hidden motivations, deep desires, and mysterious flashes of insight that dart about behind their eyes and words. They are highly complex organisms who daily face oncoming life and the possibilities of sudden death. They and their work, their play, their lives, their aspirations, are the objects of concern in the modern ministry, as here conceived. We begin with them and stay with them.

We begin with the human needs of plain people in the mood of Mrs. Browning's Romney Leigh when he says:

> That's abstract truth, I know,
> Philosophy, or sympathy with God;
> But I, I sympathize with man, not God
> (I think I was a man for chiefly this),
> And, when I stand beside a dying bed,
> 'Tis death to me . . . .
> And I, a man as men are now, and not

As men may be hereafter, feel with men
In the agonizing present.

Do not suppose for a moment that we shall leave God out
because we do not begin with Him—far from it. But a fundamental aspect of our search for true ends in the ministry is
implied in our beginning where we do; for we search induc-
tively rather than deductively, and move in our thought from
the better known to the less known, from men to God, rather
than from God to men. Until we sense the supreme significance of persons in our world, until we get them into
central focus, until they count above everything else with us,
until we are, in a word, possessed by person-mindedness, we
do not have the first prerequisite for the Christian ministry.

PERSONS AS ENDS IN THEMSELVES

What justification is there for holding thus to the supreme
significance of persons in light of all the other emphases which
have been stressed in the long history of the Christian
ministry?

The first justification lies in the fact that all persons have
uniqueness—are ends in themselves. There is a kind of
mysterious native dignity about every human being, in his
personal identity, in his potentiality for social advance as well
as for social destruction. Every human being is possessed of
unknown possibilities. A young Jewish poet who looked at
a boy in the slums of New York cried out, "You may be Christ
or Shakespeare, little child, a Saviour or a Sun to the lost
world." There is an incalculable height to human potentiality.

Every human being is an end in himself-herself, never
merely a means to the ends of someone else. Every person
believes this about himself. Fathers and mothers know this
about their children when others would exploit them—about

17

their daughters all the time, and about their sons at least in times of war. Every lover knows this about the woman he reveres "for what she is in herself." No man is merely so much labor power, merely a unit of skill for someone else to use, merely a form of investment for someone's extra resources. No woman is merely a means for the gratification of some man's desires, nor merely a mode of action—a cook or housekeeper, stenographer, clerk, or breeder of children. No child is merely a newsboy or a coal breaker, or a cotton picker, or a *merely* anything! Men and women and children with their own inherent dignity are ends in themselves as Immanuel Kant rightly called them. Human beings are actually and always to be recognized and treated as persons, as ends in themselves.

This is the basic insight that true religion has always flung into the face of greed, despotism, race hatred, and industrial exploitation, all crimes against the person, and the whole war system with its wholesale destruction of so-called enemy persons. This religious insight cries out: "There are some things you must not do to human beings. You must not scorn them nor exploit them. You must not pollute them nor degrade them. You must not blight them nor make cannon targets of them, for they are made in the image of God. Their lives are inherently sacred—they are ends in themselves." Therein lies the religious basis for an ethical imperative.

THE PERSON-MINDEDNESS OF JESUS

The second justification for finding our ends in persons, in immediate, concrete, human experience, is the person-mindedness of Jesus himself. Did anyone ever sense more clearly than He the inherent significance of persons? His essential method was to go about from person to person, to find in each of them some specific need or an open window of receptivity, and then to let into each life the brightness of that light which He Himself was. A college student said recently, "Jesus never did seem to get where He started for on His journeys. He was so often interrupted by people who needed Him, and yet He seemed always to arrive where He was to go."

Think about Jesus' method. He set up no system of government. He neither gave nor codified a system of laws. He organized no army nor roused any popular following. He enunciated no abstract philosophical system. He established no ritual of worship. He not only built no temple—He had not even where to lay His head. He set up no ecclesiastical hierarchy. And yet He made the persons whom He touched the most familiar figures of history. They represent, as in a colorful panorama, the familiar human types: Martha worried and fussy, Mary poised in a sense of enduring values, the shamed woman taken in adultery, the casual woman at the well, the baking woman with her meal and leaven, the widow and her mite, the wise and foolish virgins, the bride with her bridegroom, and His own mother—eternal symbol of motherhood. So also Zacchaeus and the lordly governor of the feast, the men standing idle in the market place, the sowers of seeds, the boy who said he would and didn't, the other who said he wouldn't and did, the boy with the loaves and fishes, the children playing in the streets, the "Pharisaic" Pharisees, Peter the impulsive, John the true, Judas the betrayer! All these common persons His touch has elevated into symbols of humanity.

This is the striking thing about the mind of Jesus. It moved always among persons, never side-tracking to secondary values. He was always putting the spotlight of His searching mind upon persons. He was always concerned for people, just as they were—their attitudes, their behavior, their mistakes and successes, their heartaches and their joys. He was somehow always quickening in them the sense of their own infinite worth and potential beauty. He came to bring good tidings to all kinds of poverty-stricken persons, release to all captive persons, sight to all blinded persons, liberty for marred and bruised and exploited persons; to proclaim a great new day of the Lord when justice, truth, and love for all persons shall be established and when God, the Eternal Person, shall be like a crown of glory, a diadem of beauty and strength to them that turn back the human battle at the gate. His person-mindedness is the justification for our own.

It was a despised man, an utterly broken man, a public prisoner, who wrote words of insight which summarize every-thing we would say about the depths of Jesus' personal concern for persons of every kind, age-long, world-wide.

There is still something to me almost incredible in the idea of a young Galilean peasant imagining that he could bear on his own shoulders the burden of the entire world: all that had already been done and suffered, and all that was yet to be done and suf-fered: the sins of Nero, of Caesar Borgia, of Alexander VI, and of him who was Emperor of Rome and Priest of the Sun: the sufferings of those whose name is Legion and whose dwelling is among the tombs: oppressed nationalities, factory children, thieves, people in prison, outcasts, those who are dumb under oppression and whose silence is heard only of God; and not merely imagining this but actually achieving it, so that at the present moment all who come in contact with his personality, even though they may neither bow to his altar nor kneel before his priest, in some way find that the ugliness of their sin is taken away and the beauty of their sorrow revealed to them.[1]

The basic concept of person-mindedness, so simple, so searching, is justified alike by the inherent nature of human personality and by the mind of Jesus himself.

[1] Oscar Wilde, *De Profundis.* By permission of G. P. Putnam's Sons.

PERSON-MINDEDNESS

SEEING PERSONS FRESHLY

If we adopt the spiritual outlook of Jesus and begin to find our ends in persons, we shall look at them with new eyes, and think more deeply about them. To think about them concretely rather than abstractly is essential—to visualize all sorts of people who are all about us in the everyday communities in which we live: "Tom" and "Harry" and "Jack," "Margaret" and "Fanny," "Aunt Susie," "Uncle Henry," and all the rest, old gray heads and bald heads, the over-serious middle-aged people, the happy-go-lucky young folks—some of whom are not so happy or lucky any more—the boys and girls, even the babies; people at all the different age points, in all the varying occupations, in all their fun, their games and squabbles, their worries, their sicknesses, their heartaches and frustrations.

These are the persons we mean, persons of first-hand acquaintance and others like them. We certainly do not mean any series of abstract entities. We must leave it to personal acquaintance and observation, to the best of the novels and the movies, to help us visualize the whole colorful panorama of persons in our present-day life. They are our job. If our ends are in their life experiences, the quicker we get at our plain business of understanding them and aiding them the better.

The lives of persons have important characteristics. They are never isolated units. There never was anyone who could live entirely alone, not even, as Yeats suggested, alone in "a bee-loud glade." For persons are always in social relationships. They are on the road or at home, in stores and offices, in grain and cotton fields, in farm barns and stock corrals, in lonely cabins in the mountains or in river bottom-lands. They are persons who live in families, in fraternities of friends, in local communities, in states and nations and social orders.

Furthermore, they are persons in changing situations. Every morning and throughout every day they face new responsibilities which they meet chiefly upon the patterns of previous behavior, patterns which trace back to causal and shaping factors deeply imbedded in their early lives. In dealing with persons we are dealing with units of the highest individuality, complexity, and mobility. They are each possessed of a personal-racial history on the background of which they face the present and rapidly changing issues of experience. To understand even one person in his life situation—past, present, and potential future—is therefore no easy matter. It is easier, in fact, to pin down an elusive philosophical concept and extract its meaning than it is to pin down and understand and clarify one person.

MANY MODERN PERSONS ARE PERPLEXED

This is largely because modern life is depersonalized. Neighborhoods that were communities where everybody knew almost everybody else are urbanized into districts where nobody knows much of anybody. Industry substitutes machines for men as fast as it can. Commerce, with its mail-order and chain-store systems, dries up the village centers of trade and friendliness. Commercial amusements in urban centers sweep even the children into crowds of atomistic little sitters, keeping them indoors on Saturdays, paralyzing their group play and their individual initiative. Many an urban family headquarters is merely a place where, and from which, individual members of a social unit which is biologically tied by sex and unescaped children temporarily come and go. Public education has become regimented into a series of rigid units which "cabin, crib, confine" lively children and creative-minded teachers. The radio imparts information, entertainment, and religion, *in absentia,* obliterating face-to-face relationships. Government is delocalized and depersonalized into bureaucracies located in distant cities where Authority sits behind innumerable smoke screens with a blueprint of standardized patterns in its hands, and the smooth-worn buck is passed from one Authority to another until the local issue is finally settled, if ever, far away by an impersonal "Higher-up."

But persons! They are unique. They are the initiators. They are the mothers and fathers, the friends and neighbors. They are the quickeners, the creative teachers, the physicians, the leaders of causes, the prophets and interpreters. How can society let itself emasculate them and cut them down to *robots?*

The climax is, of course, the military system: absolute regimentation of men as standardized units, deindividualized, numbered, and ticketed. Here are absolute commands and absolute obedience with initiative only at headquarters and not much there—officers in a higher social class, mere soldiers lower down. Persons are pawns in strategy. A death is an inconvenient incident. The news about persons and issues is systematically falsified. The purpose of the system is to slaughter enemy persons in masses as a "defense" measure. The enemies to be killed now often include babies and their mothers, refugees and the wounded in hospitals. All enemy persons count as targets—the greater the number killed the greater the victory. "Our own" people must anticipate slaughtering and being slaughtered. Conscientious objectors are ostracized and brutally maltreated. Do any ends justify these means? Or will these means destroy both persons and ends? Yet this is the accepted, mechanized, commercialized system for settling international disputes—disputes in which one person, by reason of the system, is able paradoxically to upset a world.

Such depersonalizing forces are not the only reasons for perplexity in modern life. Human beings have long had other reasons, such as accidents and diseases, earthquakes and floods, and always the old arch-enemy, death. Wild animals and wild men have long combined with physical forces to challenge man's will to life, liberty, and the pursuit of happiness.

23

His own tribe and nation have been coercive with him, inflicting rigid taboos and sadistic persecutions if he belonged to a despised race, class, or sex. Intermittent wars have been visited upon him, and unintermittent taxes. His intimates have harassed him, too, with their jangling discords and personal rancors. But until recent years he located the causes of his perplexity "out there," while "in here" there continued some sense of power to go on and win. Still free within, or feeling so, he counted in a free society.

But in a depersonalized, mechanized society a sense of impotence and futility is now upon him. His life no longer seems to him like a drama in which he as leading character shapes the plot, but rather like melodrama with the plot impinging on and nullifying the character. He also realizes more and more deeply that the causes of many of his perplexities lie within himself, and that he does not yet understand them nor how to correct them. He only knows he can no longer do the things he would. He feels he no longer counts. His open frontiers are gone. Society is an octopus— he only a midget. Unknown millions of Americans, thus bewildered, can no longer negotiate the world in which they live—not even on the simplest levels. They cannot feed, clothe, or house themselves decently nor find employment.

Yet the sense of personal worth is indispensable. One has to count somewhere. Something tragic happens to persons who are bereft of a sense of their own value—persons for whom no one seems to care. Their initiative and powers of self-direction die down. Bewilderment keeps company with them as better companions fade away. Other persons of tougher fiber or with deeper spiritual resources find ways to keep their hearts unshaken in the game of life. But vast numbers of the weak and maladjusted drag on half-alive, or sink down one by one. They show up in doctors' offices, in mental clinics and hospitals. Or they beat themselves against the void in isolated country areas or city slums and show up only in the vital statistics. The diagnoses, when there are any, are recorded as heart disease, as some pattern of retreative behavior, as anxiety neurosis, mental crack-up, "accidental" death, or suicide. The causes lie far back where they might have been treated successfully, had there been intelligent guidance and personal concern.

The causes of human perplexity and breakdown are many and varied. They are chiefly found, however, in the maladjustment of relationships among persons—in these far more than in man's relations with the physical world or the lower orders of animal life. The influence of persons upon persons ramifies throughout every aspect of human experience. Man being social to the very roots of his being has few if any perplexities which can be traced to strictly individual sources. Physical defects and other highly personal factors are present, of course, but social causation must be taken into account even there, and likewise the effects of the behavior of others in relation to such factors. Perplexed persons are pulled this way and that between conflicting loyalties and desires that are directly or indirectly social. The importance of relationships for human well being is therefore manifest. The solution of personal perplexities involves adjustments in all areas of experience and calls for social attitudes and behavior of the highest types.

CREATIVE RELATIONSHIPS OUR QUEST

We therefore meditate upon the nature of human relationships in order to sense afresh their significance. The social connections of any modern person reach afar. They extend throughout a widening series of concentric circles which center in himself. They relate him to other individuals one by one. They permeate families and all other intimate groups. They ramify throughout communities and regions far beyond face-to-face contacts. They relate him to all sorts and conditions of men. Persons are thus linked in economic and occupational groupings, in political, national, racial, and world relationships. Their most inclusive bonds are as members of the all-embracing human family.

Rightness in the quality of relationships in all these areas is of crucial importance for human well-being. At any moment the life line from one to others in even the farthest area may grow taut with mutual sufferings or relaxed by a sense of common well-being. It may be strained by hatred or quickened by beneficent good will. Cruel and exploitive attitudes brand those who have them and blight those who cannot escape their effects. Likewise with vicious relationships. Therefore, attitudes that are just and generous are indispensable if human relations are to be lifted to worthy levels. The ethical quality of the connections that blight or bless men in their associated life is indeed an index of the quality of the civilization in which they exist and which they chiefly determine. Every attitude and process that makes for high ethical quality, generous outreach, and social justice in any area of experience adds to all human well-being. Unless men are to drag on content with the status quo, the heightening of the quality of human relationships becomes the central quest for all men of good will.

What, then, are the processes that make relationships creative in the highest sense? The search for answers to that question will lead us through the four meditations that follow. Our first emphasis is upon true mutuality itself, upon togetherness as a spiritual achievement.

FOUR PROCESSES ESSENTIAL FOR
CREATIVE RELATIONSHIPS

II

ACHIEVING TOGETHERNESS

OUR pick-up points for togetherness are in brokenness—in broken families, disrupted social groups and societies, in the difficult upward climb from hostility to human solidarity. From war relationships, at the bottom of the scale, the pathway rises to the higher forms of human association. Hostilities separating those who should be able to keep the peace thrust out their ugly faces all along the way, speak in harsh words and deeds at inappropriate moments and wreck the party wherever judges, arbitrators, or conciliators are absent or unable to bring the contenders together. From the grossest and most brutal selfishness of ruthless men social progress ranges through every stage of self-interest up to just that degree of self-care necessary for the highest usefulness on the part of socially committed men. Dedication to the common good marks the noblest persons. And yet there widely prevails among modern persons a basic egocentricity which disrupts and poisons many relationships and stops the free flow of mutuality. Even though the best of persons may eventually become spiritually mature, the climb for all begins at the point of jungle behavior where self-preservation depends mainly on battle, flight, or stealth—racial progenitors of pugnacity, fugitivity, and trickery. Vestiges of these remain in all modern persons—and this, by the way, is to assert something very different from the doctrine of man's total depravity. Even persons of the most co-operative spirit often find themselves suddenly slipping down the scale into hostility and combat. The lion and the lamb may lie down together some day, and a little child may some day lead them. That certainly would be excellent. But lions are likely to behave on leonine patterns for some time yet, by reason of long living in the jungle. One dare not underestimate the length of the march of time.

Probably no other professional group in modern society knows so well the persistence of selfishness, contentiousness, and hostility as lawyers. Some lawyers, indeed, make their living by cunningly intensifying these attitudes; while others, exactly the reverse in type, make long and often unremuner-ated efforts to adjust differences, to conciliate the parties at issue, to keep cases out of court. Perhaps that is why they are called, with a certain touch of wistful idealism, "counselors at law."

If we face at the beginning of this meditation the persistence of selfishness and hostility, we shall view with clearer per-spective the tasks awaiting all who desire to live in creative relationships. But we shall also sense the importance of an-other racial inheritance which we may call primitive we-ness, or native mutuality, for that also has been a racial fact from early days.

PRIMITIVE WE-NESS AND ITS DANGERS

We-ness is in our blood, native to body, mind, and spirit alike. The long period of the dependence of the human infant has, since the beginnings of history, held some sort of family to-gether and some sort of aggregation of families or tribe. The primitive man may be wolfish, but he is not a lone wolf. Per-sons are not naturally isolational; they are relational. It is natural to scrape acquaintance, to seek a mate, to have children, to join groups, to belong to tribe or nation—gregarious as we are. Some sense of membership in the human race as a whole and in its heritage of spiritual values is natural to all persons. The roots of we-ness run deep and are ever present in human beings.

We-ness is not to be identified solely with the quick camaraderie of children, lovely as that may be, nor with adolescent attachments, prophetic as they may be. It has other times and seasons than "when good fellows get together," though these are iridescent bubbles upon its surface. It is more than all these—far more. Native we-ness permeates all relationships and supports an enormous superstructure which man has built upon it.

The beginning of wisdom in creative relationships is to recognize every present element of we-ness, to include all the common ground there is, to connect all the linkages there are, to tie in every thread. The journey toward togetherness moves on by such steps as these: to magnify sympathetic approaches, to radiate friendliness, to tighten every common bond, to deepen mutual understandings—all these lead on the way. As long as people threaten and fight one another, curse, kick, strike, and make faces at one another, the gentle desiderata of creative relationships can hardly be said to be present. As long as craft seeks advantage by tricky methods, by theft or force, by subterfuge or legal stickling, mutuality may hardly be said to be unduly magnified—at least not to such a degree as to throw the super-cautious into panic about the socializing tendencies in modern society.

Yet there are two dangers that mar our mutuality. One is the danger of underdevelopment, as in people who habitually never go halfway toward anybody else. In many persons there is a stubborn, dogged disposition to go it alone, to stick out for what they think are their own goods, their own interests, their rights and their opinions with a kind of assertive, "Brrrrrrr—watch out for me!" Such assertiveness comes out of a long racial history of competitive struggle.

Such persons at the worst are hardened individualists who yield only at gun point or under mass pressure or else are mere bluffers. In family or industrial squabbles they say, "nothing to discuss, nothing to negotiate"; or they merely walk out and bang the door. Such attitudes might be innocuous on a Robinson Crusoe island, but they are a bit out of date in any interdependent family or factory, or in national or world relationships. So also with him who says in business or property matters, "I stand absolutely on my legal rights. I neither give quarter nor ask it"—which, by the way, is war language. And so also with him who says, "Is it not enough for me to come to this conference frankly and honestly partisan, to negotiate for the best I can get for myself and my crowd? What right have you to suggest that I consider anybody's interests but my own? Life is basically competitive and partisan. Mutuality is mostly myth—grossly exaggerated in modern thinking. We are still immersed in the competitive order. I belong to the times in which I live. Co-operation can't even be tried for another hundred years." So? Danger number one, then, is an underestimate of the validity of we-ness in relationships.

Danger number two is an overemphasis on we-ness leading toward complete identification of one person with another and the subordination of the one. There is by some persons, in some relationships, a capitulation so complete that personal distinctiveness, and almost identity, are lost. In a family it is to become a compliant submissive in the hands of the family dominator—whoever that may be—autocratic father or grandfather, possessive mother or dominating grandmother, the baby, or a willful adolescent who has learned how to tantrum her way to what she wants. In a group it is to become such a grouper as never criticizes the leader or fellow-members or group policies, but utterly subordinates the self to them. Ostensibly this is done for harmony's sake, but often for the prestige of the leader, however it be camouflaged by rituals, adorned by symbols, or rationalized by exalted statements of purpose. In a political party it is to be a reliable regular, always a party yes-man, voting the straight ticket whoever is up or whatever the issue, never criticizing the boss nor believing about him the facts which are the common knowledge of others and amply verified. Such regulars habitually scorn all independents. However, they rarely scorn favoritism in their personal business connections with party headquarters. As a matter of fact, the submissive regular is the incipient grafter, if not the actual one, for his group psychology largely determines his personal ethics. In a world issue, it is to take no share in forming public opinion, but rather to drift on the surface like a bubble, inertly reflecting crowd psychology—to be but a cell in the herd mind. That delivers democracy over to fascism, and the people to the dictators. In the realm of search for enduring values it is to be a mere hero-worshiper, always slavishly to follow the hero's ideas and ardently to defend them and him. It is to give oneself over to some religious cult or to a school of thought without ever asking the antecedent or posterior questions or insisting on knowing the actual facts involved. To do that is only a little worse than always to agree with the last speaker or the loudest voice. Herein lies the danger in the doctrine of "surrender." By making a virtue of surrender, dominants lead submissives wherever they want them to go. At the worst, they do so regardless of moral principles or human values. But even when the ethical ends are genuine and worthy, the psychological dangers remain. We-ness may thus be distorted by overemphasis. The doctrine of voluntary commitment, on the other hand, necessitates discriminating thought and choice.

Despite all underemphasis and all distorted emphasis, true we-ness abides, and neither Scylla nor Charybdis shall wreck our journey toward a high togetherness which accords a true place to independence.

If native we-ness be thesis, let independence be antithesis. Independence in relationships is manifestly important, is it not? The issue may be tested for all relationships by viewing it in the most intimate—that of love and marriage. Is there rightful place for independence in love and marriage? If so, then surely there is also in all the less intimate areas. The weight of tradition is against independence in marriage, even if one omits historic eras in which husbands had power of life and death over wives, to do with them what they pleased and to put them away at will. Vestigial remains of those eras are still recorded in Christian marriage ceremonies in which the word "obey" is used and the parties to the marriage accept in word, at least, all the unknown implications of complete dominance and submission in sex, social, and spiritual relationships. Other left-over primitive elements in many marriage attitudes and conventions still credit the possession and control of women to men. Even where the pledge to obey does not pass, obedience is widely expected on the one side and the necessity of according it anticipated on the other. Yet be it remembered that not all the dominants are men. There are other methods of control than by physical force and overt commands. Who does not know that women have methods of dominating men, so subtle and skillful that many a physical giant melts under them like putty in heat? Have these methods been produced by rebellion against the arbitrary controls of men? How could women be expected never to be disingenuous, never to resort to sinuous artifices of control?

Shall the we-ness of love and marriage be sealed by rituals

and expectations which deepen and foster the dangers of dominance and such efforts to escape it?

There is a truer marriage in a meeting of equals, a marriage in which there is a recognized place for independence in the midst of mutuality. The validity of independence in marriage has its basis in the rock-bottom fact of otherness. It is further enforced by the separate biological functions, with all the profound differences between men and women which emanate therefrom. Differences in structure and function so profound could harly imply less than differences in temperament, in point of view, in experience, in attitudes, and in judgments. Are these differences to be ignored or subordinated, the one to the other? No. Not in modern creative relationships, whatever the past! Young gentlemen, beware!

Even in continuing love and marriage complete identification is both impossible and undesirable. How else than by conscious maintenance of separate identities and interests shall lovers have standing-ground from which to understand and appreciate the excellence of their beloved ones? How else shall mutual and creative helpfulness be established and maintained? To raise the issue is to answer it.

Counselors know the pathological results which follow when in marriage neurotic tendencies, exaggerated fears, hostilities, and bitterness are completely shared by a husband and wife and intensified by mutual incitement. This, indeed, is the familiar method of "working up" grievances against others to the white-hot point of explosion in bitter words or hostile deeds. Such a marriage is no marriage of true minds. It is degenerative identification, and its end is mutual dissolution of both character and marriage. Only by constructive suggestions, each to the other, by frank differences in judgment frankly expressed, if need be, can either mate be helped to the attainment of the finest attitudes and behavior within the bond. Only thus can a true marriage of true persons be carried through the wear and tear of life to creative ends.

Exaggerated independence is no less a danger than the exaggeration of identification. It, also, breaks the bond. Wherever frictions are accompanied by persistent and unrelenting self-will, wherever repentance and confession of wrong do not enter, wherever arbitrary attitudes and stiff-neckedness persist—there no spiritual communion is possible. Separations and divorces, so tragically prevalent in America, often result from such pathological independence. No marriage of true minds is possible in the midst of such attitudes. But true marriage of body, mind, and spirit is possible in human life. Countless beautiful marriages have tested these words through a lifetime of years and verified them to the very end—"to have and to hold from this day forward, for better, for worse, for richer, for poorer, in sickness and in health, to love and to cherish, till death us do part, according to God's holy ordinance." What love might be, true love hath been, indeed, and is. A high togetherness in marriage may yet be achieved without pathological identification or exaggerated independence.

So, too, in all other areas, the attitudes and processes necessary for mutuality can be sustained. Friendships can be repaired and kept on high levels. Teamwork can and does win. Group solidarity can be kept unimpaired. Church union is no chimera. International and interracial relationships worthy of Christian ideals can yet be achieved. Heaven and earth may yet be bound together. An achieved togetherness in every area is our quest. True love lifts up the symbol and is a harbinger of better days. So next comes synthesis.

TOGETHERNESS A SPIRITUAL ACHIEVEMENT

Togetherness upon worthy levels is a spiritual synthesis reaching far beyond the native we-ness upon which it is based.

ACHIEVING TOGETHERNESS

It is a synthesis of interests in which, with differences recognized, a free and voluntary commitment is made for the sake of organic, spiritual unity. Not without difficulty in any sphere, but possible in all, it is achievable in divided personalities, divided families, groups, societies, nations, and in the realm of spiritual values. It is no casual thing like a little green cap that a freshman in life plucks out of his pocket, claps on his head—and there you are! Oh no! It grows up within and between persons by means of insights and adjustments in the processes of maturing life—an interior achievement, no mere easy external adornment. To attain the synthesis of togetherness in any group relation—even if the circle include but a few persons to begin with and only gradually widen its borders—that is the first essential for creative relationships.

Togetherness always requires us to recognize that the old enemies, quick temper, hostility, and sullenness, are backtracks toward the jungle, sure symptoms of personal maladjustment. Instead of indulging these, togetherness requires us to stand the gaff when we are misunderstood or misinterpreted; to be patient under inescapable relations with frictional persons; to maintain courtesy in private and public relations alike, even in the presence of hypocrisy and deceit; to keep from bitterness when being betrayed; and, "being reviled, to revile not again," or, being attacked, to seek no reprisals. Heavy prices these are for the chance to make relationships creative. But they are incomparably lighter than the costs of unleashed hostility and war.

Habitually to show oneself friendly; to respect the bond and live up to it, even if one has to do it alone; to widen one's circle constantly by finding genuine interests in new relationships while deepening the old ones; persistently to appreciate other persons and habitually to express that appreciation—these are creative attitudes and processes. In families, this means to make all possible accommodations; to do so, it may be, with some sense of humor, with willingness to "take a joke" on oneself and to "forgive and make up"; to correct the fault which caused the "blow-off" of another, or to "back down" and ask forgiveness if one has permitted oneself the emotional extravagance of "blowing up." In groups, a creative relationship means the readiness to seek more light instead of putting in more heat, to stress the common interests, to get together, to conquer schism, to bury the past and move on with the best possible program. To maintain such a relationship in the midst of conflicting issues in economic and industrial, as well as intellectual and religious matters, it is necessary for parties at issue at least to confer, to come to agreement if possible, and if compromise without dishonor is impossible, to differ without hostility or vindictiveness. In international relations togetherness requires all parties to confer honestly and conciliate endlessly. No cards should be stacked before the conference meets; past errors must be recognized by all and actual concessions made in the search for a plan of essential justice in place of reliance on force or the sudden slaughter of civilians.

Creative attitudes and processes enter into the warp and woof of the social fabric and result in spiritual maturity. Civilization cannot endure without them. They create the spiritual values of worthy living in the ever-widening areas of life. In personal relationships they lead on the way to rich companionships, to "beautiful friendship tried by sun and wind, durable from the daily dust of life." The *Sonnets from the Portuguese* voice them on the heights of love. The rituals of fraternity are strivings toward them. The fusing of the wills of men in any bill of rights reveals them at work against injustice. Union, one and indivisible, may yet be achieved by them in any national or international life. Shared searches for truth and values in science and religion characterize the finest minds; and, war to the contrary notwithstanding, they shall yet bind the world life together in one great family of God. Their intimate epitome is in the handclasp, caress, and spiritual embrace that fuse two persons into one, but their reaches run beneficently throughout all social relations and scale the heights until they bind heaven and earth in high communion.

Difficult? Very difficult! But achievable. This is one of the points where the "mindedness" in our theme comes in. It takes intelligence to achieve true ends in creative relationships—intelligence great enough to tie one's own warring parts together in a unified personality, to attain the power of mind over feeling, to achieve emotional controls, to aid others to the same achievements, to live at peace with all men, to increase good will by every possible means, to help create a new order of justice, truth, and beauty in the great business of living. What greater uses has intelligence than these?

"Think; be sure you're right," is a motto put up on the walls of typesetters' work rooms. Why not also over every home where friction has entered, every group and society where personal antagonisms have appeared, in the chancelleries of nations, on laboratory walls, and over the study desks of all searchers for truth and the ultimate meanings of life?

What do perplexed people need so much as to use their own intelligence on their personal problems before taking them to other persons to solve or "throwing them off" on God? God and other persons are resources—yes, of course—but the use of their own intelligence, of their own problem-solving brain comes first. The attitudes and processes by which persons may handle themselves effectively in their relationships include all the insights and graces of spiritual discernment known to seers and prophets. Such attitudes and processes bring men to the supremacy of Jesus, and into temples where they, as thinking worshipers, stand in reverence before the All Highest—temples where creative relationships are born.

A PERSON-MINDED MINISTRY

It is the thesis of these meditations that Jesus plumbed the depths of creative power in relationships by His teaching and example of universal and eternal love. Therein lies His unique supremacy. That love in the lives of men and women lays hold upon all their powers, refines all the uses of the body, exalts the emotional life, and gives direction to all intellectual aspiration. We treat the teaching of Jesus at this point in relation to the world-old human tendencies to hostility and divisiveness of which we have been thinking.

Even in a tiny Galilean village in a seclusive nation where none of the modern means of swift communication were present, centuries before the consciousness of social interdependence had come, Jesus found a microcosm of relationships. By insight, social intelligence, revelation (name it as we may) He dealt with the basic problems of divisiveness and hostility.

Flashes such as these reveal the mind of Jesus: "Agree with thine adversary quickly"; "Have salt in yourselves, be at peace with one another, and whosoever shall compel thee to go a mile, go with him twain"; "All they that take the sword shall perish with the sword"; "Why beholdest thou the mote that is in thy brother's eye, but considerest not the beam that is in thine own eye?"; "Thou shalt love thy neighbor as thyself"; "Behold, I send you forth as sheep in the midst of wolves"; "Be ye therefore wise as serpents and harmless as doves"; "For everyone that exalteth himself shall be humbled, and he that humbleth himself shall be exalted"; "I say unto you, love your enemies."

Forgive? "Until seventy times seven." What a final demonstration of forgiveness He gave in His words on the cross, "Father, forgive them, for they know not what they do."

How strange this teaching seems, and new!—aeons beyond us yet. Jesus moved way out toward the other end of the scale, away from reprisals and hostility, beyond "an eye for an eye" and all the middle ground of self-interest and compromise, to the paradoxical absolute of love for enemies. At the other end of that scale He put the fact of universal love—the greatest thing in the world—regenerative creative love. What other concept is so full of sheer daring—so basically revolutionary—so profoundly true? Think of planting that principle in the midst of the military brutality of the Roman world and the hairsplitting pharasaic selfishness of the Jewish elders. "Love your enemies." Those are tantalizing words—still tantalizing to all persons in modern relationships—words which may yet win the sons of men into creative relationships that shall abide.

OUR QUEST AN URGENT QUEST

From armed hostility to universal love is a long, long road. The social behavior of any person registers his actual stage on that pathway. Every stage also in that long journey is still visible in the present behavior of various individuals and groups. Our quest, therefore, must be to observe the particular stage reached by persons, groups, societies, or nations, and to find and apply the harmonizing, peace-making efforts needed by each. Only so shall justice, truth, and love be made to prevail. The quest is a quest on many fronts. The specific issues are multiple and in all areas. Success is not always possible quickly, sometimes not at all. Hostilities must be given time to die down. Love must be long applied to some before they yield. Hence love *must be* eternal love, and between what *is* and what *may be* of love in human relationships we are to do our work. Where have ministers, ordained and unordained, a higher or more urgent quest than this? They are indeed constituent members of a fellowship of reconcilation. When was such fellowship ever so needed as now?

III

GETTING AND FACING FACTS

IGNORANCE, error, and superstition are the pick-up points for fact-getting. The massive forests of ignorance, in the midst of which the race came to awareness, still surround modern men. The unknown makes the known but a pioneer's clearing in these woods and our house of knowledge not more than a woodsman's cabin. Knowledge of practical arts first developed by reason of hunger, cold, danger, and fear. The need for food, comfort, and safety forced men to hunt for physical necessities and sheltering defenses. Dangers increased as travel extended. The arts of hunting and warfare developed. Man sought ever wider areas of operation. By land and water trails he moved to ever new frontiers. He asked the *how* and *what* and *why* of his experiences. He sought insistently the answers to the riddles of his life. Deceived by appearances, lured and defeated by hopes that failed to mature, he grew more wary, more observant, more careful with his ideas as well as his actions. He searched for reliable responses, for that which could be assured by repetition. Slowly the factual was established by testing and retesting, and ever made to serve human needs more widely. Thus he came at last to see facts as actual happenings in time or space, as events either mental or physical—occurrences, qualities, or relationships whose reality had been fully tested in experience or was inferable with certainty therefrom.

When man arrived at conscious awareness of his native

empirical method and set the stage so that he could use it with refinement under controlled conditions, and with some degree of certainty in results, scientific method was born. Both the method and the findings have widened the clearing in the woods till man now knows and uses many facts. He walks in certain areas with great assurance. And yet the forests of ignorance remain, their darkest recesses unexplored. Mysterious voices from unknown sources still whisper to him or shriek at him in the night. Unknown enemies still lurk by the trailways. Mysterious diseases steal forth to slay.

The search for reliable knowledge is as old as humanity, an ever-present and a crucial quest. It is present and crucial because man is now avid to know all about himself and the far-flung rim of the universe—their meaning and all that lies between them. Scrutiny has now turned, at long last, upon man's own nature and behavior. Psychology postdates astronomy by centuries, and clinical psychology, sociology, and the like are still in swaddling clothes. Urged on by his native curiosity man now turns upon himself and upon his perplexities the method of objective inquiry learned in his quest for certainty in the physical world about him. Persons and their life come into the focus of his search. In this area, therefore, we seek the facts most meaningful for our own meditations.

PERTINENT FACTS ABOUT PERSONS

Fact-finding in realms primarily personal and social is difficult. Facts about persons are fugitive, changeable, altered by a touch of hand, a tone of voice, or light of eyes. The searched is also a searcher. Object and subject are one, necessitating a degree of objectivity few searchers possess. As inquirers move from the more objective data of natural science to the more subjective data of the personal areas, they find it increasingly difficult to make their measurements precise. Personal data submit unreadily to fixed classifications. They are as hard to confine as mercury. They have an unpredictable way of gliding about from pigeonhole to pigeonhole, being true in one and false in another—true at three o'clock, greatly altered at four. Furthermore, fantasies that are real enough to lure men round the globe have no standing in the scientific world except as fantasies. Yet they possess in fact a strange and potent reality. Thus fantasies, paradoxically, are facts of human experience; and so are theories, imaginations, dreams, and fanciful beings like angels, fairies, gnomes, and sprites. Snow White has a little song to sing, a little word to say to all holders of narrow and rigid epistemological theories. She and her merry crew can no more be left out of reality than could Henry Ford's mental image of an automobile. Such ideas are indeed facts more potent than any dwarf or giant in the flesh or than any metal motorcar Henry Ford ever built.

What, then, are facts in persons, about persons, for persons? At the least, they must include everything which has potency in human ideation and behavior. It is difficult to run down all human data, stick pins in them as if they were tropical butterflies, classify and describe them. Some of them so alter while being chloroformed and pinned that they have already vanished before measuring tape and microscope can be applied. It is not difficult to measure the size of a dead body, but the fusion of forces that makes up the livingness of a human being cannot be completely described.

Difficulty piles upon difficulty in the application of strict scientific method to personal data. As compared with workers in the natural sciences the searchers in the more personal areas are relatively untrained, inaccurate, and often work with unsterilized hands. Wishful thinking, self-deception, hostilities, and loyalties prejudice their findings. Deceiving propaganda distort the truth. No wonder those who work with exactness in the natural sciences call the personal the "soft data" areas, unsuited to precision in method or exactness in results. They throw up their hands in despair or scorn. And yet their very absorption with impersonal data may disqualify them for judging workers or evaluating the methods in the more personal areas. Their very attitudes may become in themselves illuminating data to those at work on personal relationships.

Whatever the difficulties, the scientific spirit must carry through the process of fact-getting in the more immediately personal areas. Honest and thorough inquiry is possible there. Degrees of accuracy adequate for all practical purposes can be attained. Prejudices can be cut to the minimum. Propaganda can be exposed and ignored. Reliable results can be secured and verified.

No fact about the universe in which man lives is devoid of human meaning. Yet the leap of light to earth from the stars differs in interest from the leap of lights in lovers' eyes. Facts of immediate personal significance have the greater pertinence for these meditations. The primary interests of persons are to have our attention, and that without apologies to those who study light years and cosmic rays. Even they, being human, delight to return at times to personal facts and values, for these are of universal interest. The choice of field is, after all, a matter of volition. The spirit and method of science are not to be identified with any single area of inquiry or degree of precision to the exclusion of others. Furthermore, the scientific spirit and method have already gone far within the field of our primary interest. Results in physiology and biology, for example, are as well established as scientific findings in other fields; and the findings in psychology, sociology, ethics, and religion are not to be scorned. They make no claims to be what they are not, and they do disclose realties of the greatest human significance.

The desirable process, then, is clear: the facts about persons in their life situations must be discovered, ascertained, and made widely known. Only thus can a trustworthy basis for living in truly creative relationships be everywhere established. Facts of human import must be discovered in specific instances and with reference to particular individuals, groups, and societies. This is now possible.

The facts about any one person in his life situation can now be stated more accurately than ever before. The personal affinities, the loyalties and prejudices within a group may now be so clearly described as to serve all practical purposes. The facts about every major industrial, agricultural, or regional situation can now be assembled so reliably that a sound basis for social reconstructions is provided. It is not beyond the scope of the scientific spirit to clasify major trends in world affairs when stable social processes are not disrupted by the unpredictable actions of individuals in power. Nor is it impossible to know something about the dreams that rise out of the subsoil of life or the dreams and visions that arise by insight and inspiration. We now know much of the wind, 'whence it cometh and whither it goeth,' and what Jesus meant when He said, "So is every one that is born of the spirit." The animating ideas that shape man's inner life and social behavior are more and more clearly understood. To know everything possible about persons in their life situations with as high a degree of certainty as we may is of the essence of our quest. There is a lure about that quest, an intense interest on the part of all those who sense the significance of persons and of creative relationships in human life.

JESUS' KNOWLEDGE OF PERSONS

We do not think of Jesus as scientific in the modern sense of the word. Yet a little meditation on *scire* (to know), the root verb of science (knowledge of principles or facts), puts Him in a central place in the field of knowledge about persons.

GETTING AND FACING FACTS

It becomes evident to those who study the records of His life and teachings that He knew both the facts about the particular persons He dealt with and also understood enduring truths about the whole of human life. He seems not to have needed labored processes involving technically worded hypotheses, exactly-defined and delimited classifications, testing and verification or revision of hypotheses, the submission of data and methods to experts, and the repetition of these processes in whole or in part to establish verified conclusions in the field under consideration. His methods of knowing were evidently more direct, His insights more sure; His mind ran more freely over all data at His command. His conclusions were immediate and certain; and yet one finds no reason to suppose that He was other than keenly observant, clear in memory, skilled in analysis and synthesis, definite in conclusions, cautious in judgments, and profound in His understandings. On the contrary, His mind seems to have had these qualities along with a penetration of insight unequalled, so His disciples believe, in any other teacher.

The principles of Jesus have lived because they are true to life. They have stood the test of such scrutiny, criticism, and application to the actual problems of life, in Orient and Occident alike, as have been accorded to those of no other teacher. His principles, though rarely tested to the depths, have proved true in the lives of millions of persons throughout the centuries since He uttered them and still are vivid, creative, and prophetic in modern society. The weight of that volume of human traffic is, to say the least, evidential as to the soundness of His knowledge.

Of His teachings we shall be studying further throughout these meditations. Here we reflect on a few of His contacts with persons, one by one. Some of these occured quite without premeditation. They illustrate His gift for making a casual meeting at a street corner or a dinner party the occasion for lodging a peculiarly needed truth.

For example, He divined in the quick-witted, much-married woman of Samaria, now a bit passé and disillusioned, a deep need to learn that mere cleverness and sex pleasure as a life emphasis do not lead to increasing happiness in relationships, but mean, in fact, to choose "a single rose for a rose tree that beareth seven times seven." No wonder you're a thirsty woman. The things that last—the really important things— do not depend on being young and witty. If you could only understand! There is living water that stays fresh and sparkling up to the end of life, right on through all the later years! You might have it for the asking and never thirst again.

He found Nicodemus a flattering externalist of the professional public official type. Into his bag of political tricks spiritual realities could not enter unless the bag was turned inside out. Only a shake-up of all his methods and mental processes could shift the controls from external to interior forces. Your whole system is wrong, Nicodemus! You're so wrong, in fact, you'll have to be born all over again to get right!

He exposed the scribes as experts on catch questions—a perennial Jewish type, with all their intellectual acumen distorted into a mere game of wits—and needing to be so outwitted in their own word-splitting that realities of spiritual experience might find a mental crevice through which to enter. They needed to be told with His fine irony, "They that are whole have no need of a physician."

The Roman army officer had an unbelievable humility, accustomed as he was to the dehumanizing processes of military authority, its staccato commands, its demand for instant obedience. He was so great-hearted, so concerned about mere servants and underling Jews, that even the Jewish elders came testifying to his goodness and supporting him as he besought this strange young Healer to help him. He was a representative of Roman authority, yet he said with manifest humility, "I am not worthy that thou shouldst come under my roof." This was almost more than Jesus could stand. He marveled for joy to find a military captain with attitudes toward people so right and with such faith in Him that He turned and said to the crowd, "I have not found so great faith, no, not even among the elect."

Simon, the smug but inhospitable host who talked about his own guest behind his back—not realizing that Jesus had clairvoyant sensitivities—was such a hard-shelled old hypocrite that he could not recognize human contrition even in the presence of a woman who dared to lay aside all her feminine defenses before the faces of known puritans. Simon needed to have his adroit, sophisticate trickery smashed by straight words about etiquette, concerning which he evidently prided himself. He had to be backed into a corner and made to realize the littleness of sophistication and the largeness of forgiving love. The evidence indicates that Jesus' understanding of both these persons, sad products of urbanization, was adequate to the occasion.

By way of utter contrast He brought to light the lonely, shy, little woman, so poor, so quiet, and retreative that no one but Jesus appears even to have seen her among all the rich folks, slipping through the crowd, putting in her two tiny coins, then furtively slipping out again. She needed nothing so much in all the world as the appreciation which Jesus gave her for her persistent outgoingness.

And so it was with many another human contact: publican and Pharisee, Sadducee and Zealot, Nazarite and wine-bibber, Romans and Samaritans, soldiers and sailors, tax collectors, pious women, and even harlots (still a bit shocking, isn't it?). He seems to have known them all—known them at first hand

—"needed not that anyone should bear witness concerning man; for He Himself knew what was in man."

Furthermore, it must be recognized that according to the records, however they are interpreted, He dealt with the diseased in mind as well as in body and did it so effectively as to be unprecedentedly therapeutic and transforming. He operated on the basis of knowledge, methods, and powers that are yet beyond our understanding or command.

His knowledge of man is revealed by every contact and aspect of His life and permeates both His teaching and action. One comes to wonder, indeed, if His knowledge, instead of depending upon some mysterious, other-worldly implantation, and descending from God to man, from man to men, from general to particulars, from principles to instances, from ideas to applications, did not move in reverse order.

Might it be that his understanding of persons, developing in first-hand contacts throughout His boyhood, youth, and early manhood, was so extraordinarily acute that these contacts became the settings and quickeners of the insights which furnished the groundwork of His teachings? From instances to principles, from pertinent truths about particular persons to universal truth, from first-hand knowledge of men to knowledge of man, from empirical knowledge of man and his universal needs up and out to knowledge of God, the Answerer of human need. The High and Holy One of the Hebrew Scriptures was not the God of persons in their need sufficiently to satisfy Him; so

> He humanized God to a Father
>   And hailed Him down from above
> To yearn and serve in city streets
>   Till He hung on a cross for love.

It is well to think freshly about the mind of Christ, to seek to understand, as well as one can, His processes of thinking and knowing, rather than merely to say, "Of course He knew all things, because He was divine." This arbitrarily begs the whole question of process. Divine? Agreed, whole-heartedly agreed, because the spiritual consanguinity of human and divine is of the utmost importance to those who would pivot their thought upon the person-mindedness of Jesus. Christians get their very concept of the divine from Him.

FACING FACTS COURAGEOUSLY

The facts of life found and known, must also be faced. There are almost always enough known facts with which to work in any human situation, facts which are clues to the personal or social issue, whatever it may be. To set the most pertinent facts in array, that they may be faced intelligently, is something yet again and antecedent to the facing. Not until the facts are assembled and the diagnosis made can doctor or patient know in specific terms the condition to be faced.

People in specific situations usually have some unpalatable facts to face. They rarely like to face them. There are always facts of ill health, real or fancied, financial difficulties, loneliness, incompatibility, one's own mental quirks or past bad behavior. From these we naturally run away. Fear, flight, and camouflage persist from the racial heritage. There are strange psychological remnants still remaining from our primitive past, instinctive tendencies which are in all persons. They tempt men to take to their heels and run away from ferocious looking facts, to climb out of imminent danger like their arboreal ancestors, and then to sit in safety out on a limb and chatter about them. Such facts make other men want to hide like woodchucks in their own particular psychological holes, and still others fly away like partridges, drumming noisily. Flight is one of the most prevalent of modern sins. But to be fugitive from one's own facts is to be basically a coward. To

51

flee is often more dangerous than any of the facts from which one flees.

> Woe to him that from his burden flees!
> Crushed in the fall of what he cast away.[1]

It is singularly a mental matter not to have sufficient command over one's powers of attention to look one's own life issues squarely in the face.

Yet there is no easier or surer way to know who, what, and where one is than courageously to face one's own facts. Calmly and courageously, promptly and persistently to face reality in every life situation, in every area of life experience, is the clue to a life of power. The creative message of dynamic psychology and of the Christian religion is to face all the essential facts and all their knowable implications, to act upon all factors that are alterable by one's own action, to accept the unalterable as unalterable, to call in every available resource, and to lift one's face to the future calm and unafraid. Then, if one goes down, one will, at the last, be found to have gone down facing forward.

When bad news comes, some people cringe before it; others face it calmly.

"What is this my employer is saying to me? The company is on the rocks, our markets gone; the business closes on December 31? No other way out? All employees are being notified? And I, at fifty-five, in what I supposed was a snug berth for life—I, who never in all my years was out of work, who have secretly looked down upon the unemployed—am I out? Impossible! Not I! You can't mean I am being notified after all these years! I won't believe it! I can't believe it! I can't face it!"

"Very sorry," a calm voice replies, "we have done everything

---

[1] Francis Thompson, "Ode to the Setting Sun." By permission of Dodd, Mead & Co.

we can. We have gone over and over the situation. We have put in our all. We have borrowed to the limit. In spite of the cuts in which we all have shared, the business has shown steadily increasing losses for many months. All our reserves will be gone by December 31. That's the final day. We, too, have to face our facts. You may remember my father founded this business fifty years ago. He made it succeed. This is no easy experience for me any more than for you. It cuts to the bone to have to lay off five hundred men. My own house is being announced for sale tomorrow."

Some ministers face reality like this: "Doctor, I have a strange sensation here in my cheek; it runs deep down beneath this ugly sore which will not heal. I want the facts about it. Make your scientific tests and tell me the absolute truth. . . . . What's that you say? The tests you have made show malignant growth? The diagnosis is cancer? Cancer in my cheek? You give me but one year to live? All right, doctor, if those are the terms, I am ready." Cornelius Woelfkin, bravest of men, faced reality in those very terms. During the final months of his life, while they literally cut his face away in efforts to save him, he never whimpered once, but made every scene and every person he touched radiant by the way in which he faced reality. He himself discovered deeper spiritual realities than he had ever known before. He, like countless other men who in days long gone learned how to face reality, how to suffer, and how to die, moved on to the end triumphant, like martyr Christians in Roman arenas who died crying, *"Morituri salutamus."*

Where did they ever learn to face reality like that? From Jesus. From Him, not elsewhere. Not by stoic denials of it, not by epicurean avoidance of it, not by pagan submission to it, but by Christian triumph over it and over all the devastating facts of life. Power to face life, to live and die like that they learned and still learn from Him who steadfastly set His face to go up to Jerusalem. He well knew in light of all He had done and said that there could be but one outcome for Himself. For the suffering and death which awaited Him He was full well prepared and unafraid. He knew that He could trust Eternal Love. Neither His death nor the manner of it could have been for Him the anguishing issue. That issue could not have been in or for Himself. It must have been in and for all other persons. He had such knowledge of persons, such universal love for persons, that He knew how they might be rescued from hostility and ignorance, from fear and selfishness, from every form of wrongness, if only they knew and loved enough. He had implanted through the brief allotted years that knowledge and love in all the persons He could reach. These things He had done, but could He be sure He had set that knowledge and love deep enough into human life and into persons enough so that His message would live on through the ages? There was the anguishing issue! Would the new realm come or would it fail to come? Would the cause fade out? Would enough persons understand and care? Or would the light die down in the hearts of His own men, like a fire blazing not yet hotly enough to carry its own heat to conflagration? Witness the burden visibly on Him through all the action of the last days in Jerusalem, breathing through all the intercessory prayer for them, voiced again and again at the Last Supper, when contention, betrayal, and denial broke bread with Him at His own board and must have well-nigh broken His heart. But through to the end—through accusation, travesty of trial, buffoonery, scourging, mob passion, treachery, and final desertion—through to the end He went, triumphantly facing it all and saying finally, "Father, forgive them, for they know not what they do. . . . . Into Thy hands I commend My spirit." Almost the last words He heard from human lips were words of raillery that must have sealed His assurance of ultimate victory: "He saved others,

Himself He cannot save." "He saved others, Himself He cannot save." He is where men and women learn how to face reality, how to suffer, how to die, and how by death itself to communicate life.

All the great experiences of life are common to all men. Soon or late one learns that every person has someday to face reality upon some level of experience, and that ultimately reality has to be faced upon every level and in every area of life. "Whatever happens to another happens to oneself, and if you want an inscription to read at dawn and at nighttime, and for pleasure or for pain, write up on the walls of your house in letters for the sun to gild and the moon to silver, 'Whatever happens to oneself happens to another.'" [2]

The way in which persons face their facts is the crucial issue! Those who face them calmly and courageously upon the highest levels learn that not all their facts are problem facts. They discover that not all facts crash in upon them from without, that some are resource facts, that inner resources are also facts. Spiritual realities emerge within and wait wistfully to be used by persons who sit perplexed about their hearthstones pondering what to do. These inner resources must be self-released into action and utilized for the solutional power that is in them.

Artists, however poverty-stricken, often discover unrealized abilities in themselves; and through them spiritual resources are released to others, sometimes with a glad surprise. "These blue dabs I made on my canvas yesterday took on, as I worked, the semblance of a mountain lake surrounded by snow-capped peaks, and above and beyond them the infinite blue of the sky. Today men came and stood silent before it, then quietly said they found there an answer they had been seeking for their needs. They had long yearned, they told me, for a deep

[2] Oscar Wilde, *De Profundis.* By permission of G. P. Putnam's Sons.

blue lake of peace like that, within their own souls, and this lake with the skyey blue of its waters (I dare not call it mine) was to them an answer."

William Ellery Leonard says it all poignantly in his "The Sculptor," intimating problem, attitude, resource, and high result:

> I wrought unaided save
> By wind and wood and wave,
> And night and Mars the red,
> And poets dead.
>
> No man from sun to sun,
> Seeing me, said, "Well done";
> No woman smiled and chose
> For me a rose.
>
> But thus my arm at length
> Did win a silent strength—
> Thus here the statue stands
> For all the lands.[3]

It is part of his literary subtlety to throw the spotlight upon unaided man, as if the individual and his creative powers were all, but then to say, by indirection, that he wrought *aided* by wind and wood and wave, by the night sky and by poets dead. In other words, he was not alone in his loneliness—unaided in his impotence. The universe was with him—profoundly so—and that is one of the great contributions that religion brings to perplexed people, that Christianity presents to psychology. Life and its therapies are more than descriptions of mental states or the adjustment of mental mechanisms. The universe works with those who face reality upon every level and in every area of relationship. This also is a fact of

[3] William Ellery Leonard, "The Sculptor," from *The Vaunt of Man.* Copyright 1912. By permission of The Viking Press, Inc., New York.

life to be reckoned on. There is a cosmic reference in all that they are or do, and every common bush is all "afire with God" to those who sense the reality of their cosmic resources.

THE CRUCIAL IMPORTANCE OF TRUTH ABOUT LIFE

What could be more important than the facts about people, the distinguishing, pertinent facts? What could be more significant than the truth about human life, specific and general knowledge upon which true interpretations and problem-solving actions can alone be based? Yet it is at this very point that the inadequacy of our information and the immaturity of our common attitudes appear. It is precisely in the matter of information about persons and our knowledge of the meanings of human experience that modern persons are so faulty. It is in these particular areas that irresponsible tales, rumor, and overt distortions of the truth are prevalent. Incalculable damages to persons result.

So also with belief in magic, fortune-telling, soothsaying, astrological and phrenological bunk, the supersitions of farmers' almanacs. These permeate the psychological subsurface life of great sections of America and are not absent from powerful circles in the business world. A hundred kinds of quacks live luxuriously by lying ingeniously. There are also the palpably false beliefs of many religious cults which thrive on the credulity of emotionally starved people. Many of their superstitious beliefs have come straight from primitive jungles, are hoary with age, and have been disproved a thousand times. These prevail, however, far more widely in America than the intelligentsia who live provincially in the centers of culture are aware. Many of the searchers who have shared the studies out of which this book has grown know these at first hand in the human subsoil of their parishes; but they also know that such false beliefs are not limited to the colored race, nor to migrant laborers, nor to the sharecroppers and wage hands of the cotton states. They know the slum beliefs of San Francisco, Chicago, and New York, and the wide prevalence of secreted superstitious fears. It is dangerous to overestimate the degree to which distorted beliefs about life have been eliminated from American consciousness by the much-heralded dissemination of modern scientific knowledge. Even the intelligentsia, in recent years, have been annoyed to discover how many fossil remains lie buried in their own psychological subsoil.

Nor are these the only areas where fact-getting and fact-facing are essential. In the going practices of such social agencies as the press and the theater the truth about life is so often suppressed and distorted as to make unbiased objectivity a wistful hope rather than an established reality. The press, agent of public information, vehicle of facts from producer to consumer—surely the press has attained accuracy, freedom from bias, justice to producer and consumer alike. Has it? In a home where tragedy has come, does the reporter seek the facts as they are? In a sense he does if he represents not dirty yellow but decent journalism. Yet in another sense, and basically, he does not. Following his "nose for news," he ferrets out the dramatic factor and distorts the story to play it up, caring not how devastating to the persons involved may be the publicising and distorting of intimate details or those departures from the true proportions of fact which falsify the truth. More than this, our searchers know well the sinister power of advertisers and of commercial interests to suppress and distort the news. Publishers have fought valiantly and rightly for freedom from political controls. Often, however, they lack the social maturity and courage to tell the truth about human life as it is, and thus fail to serve the ends of social justice.

The governmental suppression and distortion of news in wartime brings to climax this most dangerous practice of tampering with the truth. Censorship of the news adds willful perversion to a process already more than difficult. It is the acme of distortion of the facts about persons, nations, and events. Lies shatter the foundations of national integrity and rob the people of confidence in the agencies of information, in the government, and ultimately in their corporate life itself.

So, too, in regard to dramatic misrepresentation of the truth about life. Twenty-five years ago the author wrote the following words he has never seen reason to retract. With the attendance at motion pictures now well-nigh universal, their importance has indeed been greatly magnified.

The present situation throughout the dramatic group indeed is characterized by widespread misrepresentations of the human story. Scores of popular plays do not tell the truth about life. They do not present an accurate picture of human experience. The satisfactions permitted by playwrights to their characters could not be known by them in life itself. The results of human action as portrayed are not the results of such action as experienced. The audience is therefore led to generalize falsely about the laws of human life. For example, a life of license is pictured as a life of liberty and joy. Remorse and the broken years are obscured. Thus infidelity is made to seem "not so bad," even "justifiable under certain conditions." The blasted child and the life-long suffering are permitted to be forgotten. The picture is simply not a true picture.

Audiences are everywhere tempted to believe a variety of lies about life such as these: "Happy are they who follow their own desires now, for they shall taste all the joys of life." "The love of money is the root of all roses." "Cleverness covers a multitude of sins." "Blessed is he who gets away with the stuff." The theater is responsible for persuasive portrayals of a host of lies like these, and in no small measure for their wide acceptance among the people. . . . .

The playwright and actor who join in this malicious attack upon faith in human virtue, and who trick an audience into confusion about the laws of life, have done an evil thing, for the truth about life is the most priceless asset of the human race, long lived for and died for by noble men and women. Nothing is more sacred. Our lives depend upon it. The fabric of civilization is wrought of it, and when men and women believe lies in place of it, the social order rots out.[4]

THE TRUTH IS A SACRED TRUST TO MINISTERS

To all thoughtful citizens the truth about persons is crucially important. To whom is it more so than to ministers? To them it is a sacred trust. To know and to face and to speak the truth is certainly one of the prime obligations laid upon them. People want the truth. Despite all their sensitivities, their camouflages and concealments, people want and must have facts.

When a mother is ill, what the family want is not honeyed words from doctor or minister, vague optimism or routine talk that actually amounts to lazy-minded evasion. They want intelligence and concern—and each of these from both men. They want from the doctor accuracy of diagnosis and prescription, blood transfusion or oxygen tent—whatever is necessary—and that without an hour's delay. They want from the minister intelligent attention with genuine personal concern. They want courageous hope based on faith in God and man, faith that has faced both life and death and knows the triumph of love over death as an established fact. From their minister they want the truth about life and death and his honest grounds for faith in the power and continuance of eternal love. A doctor who will not study hard to learn the truth about disease and health is not allowed to practice in most states. Why should he be? And why should a minister who will not do his utmost with open mind to divest himself

[4] Richard Henry Edwards, *Christianity and Amusements*, Association Press, New York, 1915, pp. 50, 51.

of ignorance and error and find the truth about life? Through all their experiences people crave the truth. They know it is the truth that maketh them free.

This, then, is our second great essential basis for creative relationships: to get and to face, in every area of life experience, the pertinent facts as facts.

REALIZING THE MEANINGS OF FACTS

HASTE AND SUPERFICIALITY BALK REALIZATION

OUR third essential has its pick-up points in haste and superficiality. Men were built for action, with contractile muscles, flexible joints, and nervous resilience. They have a long activist history in combat and flight, in physical work and play, in travel by land and sea. Moderns are therefore quick on the trigger, often jumpy. This is especially true of persons from Anglo-Saxon and related stocks, who live in the stimulating cold of northern latitudes; but it is basically true of men generally, and, sufficient stimulus being given, is visible even in the most phlegmatic persons. Motor responses to the dinner bell on any Southern plantation bear witness.

Man's predisposition to action has been played upon by innumerable devices for speeding up his working powers, quickening his play impulses, or rushing him into hasty decisions. How could he, being what he is, altogether avoid haste and superficiality under the stimulation of such devices? Many moderns strangely enough seem to act on impulse even more than wary primitive men. Some Americans have specialized in scorning traditions, conventions, and inhibitions to such a degree that social controls have little meaning for them. Thus native impulses step out naked or but lightly filmed and then rush in where angels fear to tread.

There is a type of youth psychology widely prevalent in America which is vigorous and rightly impatient of outworn ways. But it is wrongly scornful of the past as a whole and undiscriminating among difficult present issues. It is inconsiderate of personal values as others treasure them, and is lacking in courtesy and good taste. Such young people neither face nor realize any but the most superficial facts. They discuss with high emotional fervor the contrasting abilities of commercial dance orchestras and the latest thing in jazz. They are victims of the modern mania for speed, flare, and sex stimulation. They illustrate the results of commercializing play into amusement. They exhibit emotional instability, crude selfishness, and essential immaturity despite their superficial sophistication. Fortunately most American young people are not thus afflicted, but there are enough who are to point a trend.

This youth type has a psychological relative known in the family as "Uncle Charlie," who in public is the great American extravert executive. In his working hours he is always terrifically busy—all pepped up for hustle. He speeds up everything and everybody. He takes on many jobs at once, has several secretaries to get his facts for him, never having time to investigate for himself, and keeps several lawyers to face them for him, since they understand the issues better than he. Yet "Uncle Charlie" prides himself on taking "unhurried time" to study the issues and to realize what they involve while he flies from Chicago to Oklahoma City every Tuesday afternoon. He covers so much landscape that he rarely stays put anywhere any more. He has so many ideas supplied him by others that he never digs down into real dirt for himself at all. Magnificent "Uncle Charlie," one of the "big guns" who rule America, but who picks his best ideas off the top of the pile where his astute little private secretary puts them. Despite all his sight-seeing, he hasn't taken one really good look at himself for years, to find who, what, and where he is in the common life of which he is a part. If he were forced to entertain such a laborious thought as that, he would doubtless order a cocktail instead, or read some set of resolutions passed in his praise by a group of his cronies.

It is no wonder that structures built by such men of super-speed—structures of business and human relationships—do not stand the test of time. Innumerable collapses in the depression are too lately with us to necessitate many examples such as Bing's island castle, never finished in spite of the squandered millions, or Bang's folly mansion on the avenue with plans changed seven times while building, until the whole disjointed pile was scrapped by its self-disgusted owner. Waste and collapse are sure to follow the haste and super-ficiality of such adolescents.

Americans like these, young or old, are quite unconscious of the quiet processes of normal growth that show first the blade, then the ear, then full corn in the ear. They have never heard of the spiral arc of growth, in which meditation normally follows upon actions already taken—a period of reflection followed in turn by new action bettered by the reflection, and that improved action followed in its turn by the renewal of quiet meditation. This is the rhythm of normal living, thoughtfully turning backward, thoughtfully turning forward. Such rhythm checkmates haste, diminishes error, and puts an end to superficiality.

These two aspects of the spiral arc of growth are the clues to our essentials three and four. Number three has to do with realizations born of meditation, prayer, and seasons of quiet. "In returning and rest shall ye be saved; in quietness and in confidence shall be your strength." Realizations born of reflection—these are seen as preparation for more intelligent action when again the time for action comes.

REALIZING THE MEANINGS OF FACTS

Awareness lags behind events, yet largely depends upon first hand sense preceptions. Conscious awareness of the meaning of an event seems always to trail behind the event. As in the case of a burn or wound one does not suffer in the first instant as acutely as afterward, so full awareness of meanings is a slow traveler that rarely comes promptly and sometimes never comes at all. The physical basis of this fact lies in the mechanisms of sense perception. The communication systems of the body-mind are relatively slow-speed instruments. Their messages are often clouded by emotional static and fatigue. Yet deep awareness depends in high degree upon first-hand sense perceptions. Direct sense perceptions are *realizers,* i.e., agents of realization, makers of reality in consciousness—a concept we shall use frequently hereafter in these pages.

The limitations of the body-mind must be taken into account. Facts of first-hand sense perception are more quickly realized than second-hand facts—especially repugnant sights and sounds, odors, flavors, and contacts. Epistemological battles still rage over the degree to which knowledge is dependent upon direct sense perception. Into that issue we cannot enter here, save to recognize that facts at a distance—unseen and unheard or seen and heard at second hand—are less vivid in consciousness than facts directly perceived. This is true despite all that radio, motion photography, and sound photography have presented to the eye and ear. The facts they present do not have the same vividness as facts seen and heard at first hand, for there is a strange lack of verisimilitude about them. They are not felt to be one's own facts. They lack the stimulus to action which is present when facts are near enough to see, touch, hear, taste, and smell. Movie scenes do not smell (at any rate, not so much as they used to), nor can one clasp hands with a radio speaker nor talk back to Hitler. A captain of trench mortars once said he preferred trench mortars to rifles, bayonets, or machine guns because he did not have to see what happened when he made a hit in the middle of a mass of troops. So it is that long-distance sins and devastations wrought by the heads of ruthless corporations, operating chiefly from Chicago and New York, are easier to commit, and their social consequences harder to realize than close-up brutalities. "Long-distance sinning" is one of America's favorite patterns of behavior. The physical senses are powerful agents of realization; and when the great American exploiters are somehow made to see, smell, and hear at first hand the devastations they have wrought upon tragically helpless persons in out-of-the-way places, there will be fewer complacent men sitting in luxurious urban offices waited on by servile boys in immaculate uniforms.

The crucial questions of realization have to do with the degree of social awareness at which any person arrives, and whether, when awareness comes, it is made the basis of constructive changes in his behavior.

Realization asks who, what, and where am I? Those who learn some measure of mental control over impulses also learn how to tone down their tendencies to haste and superficial action. They learn how to live calmly beneath the tossing surfaces of life, how to face their own facts and the social consequences of their behavior, how to reflect courageously and constructively. They begin to realize who, what, and where they are. They follow the trail of meanings. Deeper realities within the self and values that are real to others emerge into consciousness. Then comes a profound sense of responsibility which is normally the seat of dynamic change. Clarity of insight comes as well as a fresh understanding of the lot of others. When realization as to who, what, and where one is comes clearly into the sunlight, then there is perspective for intelligent living and informed social action in the modern world. A high self-direction, utilizing all one's resources for human welfare, becomes less difficult. Creative relationships are more readily achieved.

There are bypaths that lead aside. One path leads into the

swamps of morbid introspection, self-blame, isolation, and melancholia. Another leads to the jagged ledges of hard criticality, to attitudes of superiority, to the blaming and exploitation of others. But a straight ascent upon which one climbs a bit, rests and thinks a bit, and climbs again—the ascent of healthy mindedness—is possible for all. Clear views in morning sunlight are attainable by all persons who care enough to pay the price of self-discovery for the sake of creative relationships. How does one arrive at the deeper meanings of the facts he has gotten, assembled, and faced? How does one realize and accept not only the factness of his facts but also their far-reaching implications for himself and others? There are many agents of realization. To some of these we now proceed.

Time flight is a realizer. Old Father Time is inexorable despite wishful thinkers who, like Joshua of old, try to stay his march across the heavens. Neither the tinkering of Congress with its clocks nor daylight-saving devices alter the sun-directed march of events. The old gentleman, however crotchety, still wields his scythe to the fraction of a split second. He is the progenitor of all events. Humans are ever slow to realize that, compared with his exactness, their time sense tends to find the hour always later than they think it is.

In primitive life, events broke in like this: to hear in the deep of the forest an unfamiliar sound, to listen intently, to move cautiously toward its apparent source, to see from a height a band of strange warriors gesticulating stealthily, to feel the imminence of the attack—these could be sensed in a trice, the warnings given, the defenses raised. But to realize the meanings of pillage, rapine, and slaughter, abduction of women and children—these took a long, long time, if indeed the full meanings of such events could ever reach the depths of the consciousness of any person, group, or tribe. Consciousness is ultimately self-protective and is finally incapable of further suffering or realization.

In modern life it may come like this: a petulant raid in South Africa, the sinking of a battleship at Santiago, the assassination of an Austrian archduke, the extortionate demands of an Oriental military clique, the decision of one man to take what he wants though he send a world again to war. The repercussions of such events bring some minor realizations quickly, send American housewives scurrying to corner groceries before the price of sugar rises by a penny—but the meanings for human destiny of a world war who can realize? Not we. Not yet. Not for generations!

Events still break in upon men as they always have with unexpected suddenness and frequency. There is a strange naive simplicity of expectation about humanity still, a sort of native wistful trust in the ongoingness of life in its familiar channels. Habituations play their part in this. Poverty, lack of knowledge of conditions beyond the nearest horizon, lack of imagination, lack of a car or carfare still hold the vast majority where they are. In spite of economic depressions or volcanic eruptions, in spite of wars and rumors of wars, most people work on in their habitual ways, in their accustomed places. Farmers farm on the slopes of Mount Vesuvius and in the bottom lands of the Mississippi delta, though they know well enough their risks. In spite of the modern exodus for summer and winter vacations and all the vast migration of modern laborers, localism and habituation are still in predominant control. It is still news in the local paper, about most of us, that we are away from home rather than at home. And even though many Americans circle the globe, they are far from being world-minded or up-to-date with themselves. Indeed, it is reported that even swank American tourists are still at points naive, with their native habitats locatable by accent if not by clothes. Many a modern tractor farmer, plowing old mother earth with a set of twenty plows, still treats his wife with a twenty-mule mind. Thus events outstrip mental changes. Events break in suddenly upon nests of fancied security. They are still the primary agents of realization. They wake persons up in the night with cries of fire or flood. Events, as in melodrama, still impinge with dramatic suddenness upon the actor. They hold him up and say, "Who, what, and where are you? Why are you where you are?"

The melodramatic aspects are not all. True drama still persist in human affairs. The leading character can still shape the plot. Persons can still use events as instruments of realization. Vast world happenings can be made to deepen man's understanding of the forces that play upon his life and therefore tell him something of who and where he is. He may learn habitually to say, "I have got to make everything that has happened to me good for me."

The forces of nature, such as rain, hail, wind, fire, drought, and pestilence, may be made to serve as agents of spiritual realization. Illness, accidents, the loss of goods and much-loved friends may be used by persons to deepen awareness, to release them from their localisms and habituations, to universalize them. Thus they learn that "whatever happens to another happens to oneself" and "whatever happens to oneself happens to another." So time flight and meaningful events serve as realizers. They deepen man's awareness of the universal and of the essential nature of human experience.

Sins are realizers. Man has long been hardened to the rough weathers of time and chance that come upon him from without. But the citadels of his life are often more vulnerable to treachery from within than to external attack. His sins betray him. His Achilles' heel is in his psychological vitals, not in his bodily extremities.

It is a characteristic of modern superficiality to suppose that

69

wrongdoing, awareness of it, and repentance for it are no longer in order in polite society. The sense of sin seems indeed to be sharply diminishing in modern life; but none the less, sin is widely present, however denied and camouflaged. Many persons are in utter confusion as to what sin is, having lost their norms of rightness, their standards of behavior. They do not know whether to think of it as some departure from known and socially accepted standards of conduct or as transgression against the laws of God, or not to think about it at all. Yet in the deeper levels of consciousness the earlier patterns upon which they were trained in childhood continue to reassert themselves. And the laws of the land, though frequently changed, still peg responsibility for private as well as public actions upon particular persons for particular deeds branded as crimes and misdemeanors. Hence, the consciousness of wrongdoing abides. The moral structure of American life is still fundamentally intact. Despite its changing fringes, it is based on historic human experience, which does not greatly change. To those who have been trained in religious homes, sin carries still the connotation of an offense against the Eternal Source of stability and rectitude.

The classic account of sin, ever since Jesus gave it, has been the story of the younger brother whose impulses confused his ideas and robbed him of his normal relationships. That story vividly portrays the processes we are studying in these four chapters. Step by step the drama of man's fall and recovery is epitomized.

And he said, A certain man had two sons: and the younger of them said to his father, Father, give me the portion of thy substance that falleth to me. And he divided unto them his living. And not many days after, the younger son gathered all together, and took his journey into a far country; and there he wasted his substance with riotous living. And when he had spent all, there arose a mighty famine in that country; and he began to be in want. And he went and joined himself to one of the citizens of that country; and he sent him into his fields to feed swine. And he would fain have filled his belly with the husks that the swine did eat: and no man gave unto him. But when he came to himself. . . . .[1]

That is realization—"When he came to himself." It was as if he had been a long time absent from his true self, separated from it, as indeed he had been; then, unexpectedly, he met himself again where he (a Jew) was keeping company with degrading swine. Suddenly realization came, awareness of who and what and where he was—his father's son, lost from home and all relationships, living like a hog, no meanings left in life, not even husks for his physical hunger. "When he came to himself, he said . . . . I will arise and go to my father." Even though sins, like chameleons, change their appearances just enough to match the colors of the modern moment, as if they were really fresh young things instead of ugly old hags rouged up again, human nature has changed little since Jesus told that perfect story.

Let us now look at four pictures of sin in four different areas of life experience. These four confessions are all up-to-date and all within the personal experience of our searchers. They reveal human nature as essentially unchanged and the consciousness of sin as a vivid, present reality. They are all of them sins against persons. Such sins, when seen for what they are, become agents of realization.

"I was driving home alone late after a party, having left my date at her house. I must have been driving pretty fast on what I thought was an open road. It was somewhat misty, as I remember it, and I know I was getting sleepy. Suddenly I felt the car jolt. I saw something sort of slide away into the

[1] Luke 15:11-17.

mists and make a funny sound. Before I knew what I was doing, I stepped on the gas and beat it for home—speeded her up and kept right on till I got there. I knew I ought to have stopped instantly, but a queer feeling got hold of me. Something inside of me said 'Get away, get away, get away!' When I got home I went right to bed. . . . . The second day afterward the officers came and asked to see me and my car. On the right front fender they found a little piece of a boy's suit of clothes, some blood stains, and a shred of underwear. They matched them up with those on the body of the boy. I had hit him with my fender. A farmer found him dead by the side of the road next morning. It was his own boy. . . . . Well, I'm a hit-and-run driver, I am. That's what I am—a murderer, according to law. My God, I wish I'd stopped instead of stepping on the gas! It all happened so fast! Do you suppose I'll ever get out of jail again?"

Here is another picture of a man who waked up too late. "I started out by shading the truth a bit in what I told my wife. I did it to begin with as a sort of courtesy to make things easier for her. I soon found it suited my convenience, now and then, to shade it a little more. That let me do what I wanted to do, and I had my fling while her third baby was on the way. I only twisted the facts a little at first; but as things went on, I got more and more careless; and when her labor pains started earlier than anyone expected, they hunted the town over for me and found me where I was—you know where I was and the kind of a house it is. How could I ever have gotten there—with my wife about to bear me another child? My God, what sort of a skunk am I anyhow? I know the law can't touch me, but how can I ever look decent people in the face again? Her silence cuts me more than if she'd cut me down as she ought to. That baby is a torture to me. I can't stand it! If I had only waked up earlier!"

There is an awareness that lies deeper than calculation. "I

started very quietly putting the pressure on, a little at a time, eight per cent and payment on the exact date the notes were due, not a day of grace. That's the legal rate with us, and payments must be made as agreed. I had never promised to extend the notes if he couldn't pay, and when he begged for time something happened inside of me. I've always wanted money more than anything else in life; so I screwed him up to ten, and then to twelve, and finally to sixteen per cent. I said to myself, 'The risk is great. I must be protected. Double the legal rate is none too much for me! I wish I'd waked up before he committed suicide, with that note he couldn't meet lying before him. Everybody knows now I'm a usurer. I know I am responsible. People are calling me hard names. I'm really a murderer. And I'm a trustee in a Christian church. My God, what am I anyway?"

Business success is not always accompanied by social awareness. "Over and over again I said to them, 'No siree! I won't meet those fellows who claim to represent my men. This is my factory. I built it. I made it pay. I made my fortune out of the profits from it. I built this house and educated my children out of it. I built this great new building out of it. Nobody else ever sweated his life out for this business.' . . . . Questions? Sure, I'll answer your questions. . . . . Well, some of the men have been here a long time—thirty years is the longest—most of them have been here five. Any pension system? No, I never could afford it. Any unemployment provisions? No, the government provides for that; they average 221 days a year. Hours? Eight. The law requires eight now. We used to work ten and twelve. Wages? Twenty-five cents an hour, two dollars a day. Does a man get $442 a year, then, on the average, to support his family? Yes I guess it would figure out about that, but there are usually two workers to a family, sometimes three, so they come out pretty well. Saftey provisions? Well, I am

73

planning to improve them. Sanitary arrangements? Those, also, the government inspectors have been after me about lately, I admit. Have I ever permitted any kind of a union? Not on your life, and never will! Their demands are always exhorbitant. How much is the strike costing? Well, I haven't reckoned up, but it's an awful lot—detectives, strike-breakers, damages to property, lost production—it costs big money to fight 'em. . . . . Well, maybe I'm wrong. Maybe they wouldn't have struck if I'd given them thirty cents. Maybe we could have worked it out without warring about it. What I can't stand is to see their women and children starving—just plain starving. And the men—they are really my men, although they don't think I care a thing about them. . . . . Well, if they'll agree to play fair, maybe I'll talk with them."

Mental quirks are realizers. Back of most sins there lies some mental quirk, though mental quirks are not to be thought of as sins. The spotlight of inquiry has now been put upon varied forms of behavior until certain patterns are as well known as measles. When any person's habitual reactions are seen in behavior terms, clues to who and what the person really is are given. Such clues always lead to some spot in the life which is where he is. Characteristic ways of behaving are among a person's most distinctive marks. To study the behavior, the mind-sets, and especially the mental twists of other persons is to see characteristics which affect their relationships. This makes one realize that any man might well observe his own attitudes and habits carefully. He might discover some quirks he had not realized.

Does one habitually rush about like a bumblebee, here a little and there a little, always resounding noisily, exhibiting action without direction, always going yet never arriving—the kind of man who, when he doesn't know what to do, generally does he knows not what? If one is like that, and if some fair spring morning, while compelled to wait for a flat tire to be repaired, he could see himself as objectively as others see him, self-realization might ensue. Surely this man's sense of humor would rescue him from morbid introspection, and his attitudes in his relationships would never be quite so bumbly again.

Does one in the face of difficult situations habitually retreat from them into his shell, refusing to start his motor at all or, if compelled to drive, make for some sequestered nook well off the main highway? Does he always, when he can, avoid and evade and run away into an inner chamber where the world and all its complexities and especially all the bumblebees and all the great American extravert executives are left behind? If one were to discover he had become that sort of person, his meditations in the inner chamber might bring him to realize that he had better get himself up and out into action. The answer is for him to face reality. That would alter his relationships profoundly.

Does a lady habitually dissolve in tears? Is she showery in her responses to strain rather than peppery, brittle, or crumbly? Does she tend to disintegrate in a series of rainy reactions without ever drying out sufficiently to look her situations straight in the face dry-eyed, clear, and well controlled? Does she all too frequently water the domestic garden instead of building reservoirs of patience and high control against the rainy day? If she only had a little shaft of dry humor in her kit to turn on herself some rainy night, she might realize that most people do not like to be wept on too often. That realization might change her relationships quite a bit.[2]

Enough! Even the dominants and the submissives, even the self-blamers and the blamers of others, the exhibitionists and the camouflagers, the alibiing rationalizers and the meticulous perfectionists, the inferiority sufferers and the monocle-wearers of superiority—if they could but realize, if they could but laugh a little at themselves, how their relationships would change! They may need help from other people, but they must have help from themselves in order to face their

[2] Richard Henry Edwards, *The Place of Persons in the Educational Process*, privately printed, 1932, p. 9.

own facts and to realize the meanings of them to all concerned. That way lies sanity. Mental quirks, if not too quirky, may be agents of realization. Objectively to see one's own idiosyncratic self alongside of other almost equally humorous persons helps to uncover who, what, and where one is. Neither advanced neurotics nor psychotics can do this—that is one of the tests.

Friends are realizers. A friend realizes the gifts and limitations of his friend. True friends help their friends to realize who they really are. Matthew Arnold puts it thus:

Only—but this is rare—
When a beloved hand is laid in ours,
When, jaded with the rush and glare
Of the interminable hours,
Our eyes can in another's eyes read clear,
When our world-deafened ear
Is by the tones of a loved voice caressed—
A bolt is shot back somewhere in our breast,
And a lost pulse of feeling stirs again.
The eye sinks inward, and the heart lies plain,
And what we mean, we say, and what we would, we know.

A man becomes aware of his life's flow,
And hears its winding murmur, and he sees
The meadows where it glides, the sun, the breeze.

And there arrives a lull in the hot race
Wherein he doth forever chase
That flying and elusive phantom, rest.
An air of coolness plays upon his face,
And an unwonted calm pervades his breast;
And then he thinks he knows
The hills where his life rose,
And the sea where it goes.[3]

[3] Matthew Arnold, "The Buried Life." By permission of The Macmillan Co.

REALIZING THE MEANINGS OF FACTS

Suffering is a realizer. Of all the agents of realization, suffering is the most potent, though not all sufferers grant such agency to their suffering. Only a tiny portion of the vast incalculable mass of it in human experience is made to serve high ends, but that tiny bit illumines the possibilities. Broken bodies, shattered nerves, crushed spirits, physical pain, mental anguish and spiritual frustration are to some degree in the lot of all men. They may break morale, deplete resilience, and wreck relationships. At the tragic bottom end of unresolved suffering lies death by suicide or murder or both. But the upper reaches of the pathway for those who come to awareness with the help of Eternal Love finally move out of darkness into sunlight on high places.

There is an ancient message in the Hebrew Scriptures that voices this: "Comfort ye, comfort ye, my people, saith your God. Speak ye comfortably to Jerusalem; and cry unto her, that her warfare is accomplished." And this: "When thou passest through the waters I will be with thee; and through the rivers, they shall not overflow thee: when thou walkest through the fires, thou shalt not be burned, neither shall the flame kindle upon thee. For I am the Lord thy God, the Holy One of Israel, thy Saviour."

The words that follow have been chosen to convey the meaning of suffering of a different type than the forms of suffering more frequently receiving attention. These are words written in an English prison by a man of acute sensitivity, a publicly branded sinner, still scorned and hated by a certain type of so-called "righteous" person—his very name, Oscar Wilde, utterly tabooed by some of them. These words have been chosen with the hope that they may some day come under the eyes of some boy in prison, bring him light in his dark loneliness, assurance that he is never alone and that there are those of us outside the walls who suffer with him and bear him in our hearts, whatever it might have been that brought him to prison.

I have got to make everything that has happened to me good for me. The plank bed, the loathsome food, the hard ropes shredded into oakum till one's finger-tips grow dull with pain, the menial offices with which each day begins and finishes, the harsh orders that routine seems to necessitate, the dreadful dress that makes sorrow grotesque to look at, the silence, the solitude, the shame—each and all of these things I have to transform into a spiritual experience. There is not a single degradation of the body which I must not try and make into a spiritualizing of the soul. . . . .

When first I was put into prison some people advised me to try and forget who I was. It was ruinous advice. It is only by *realizing* what I am that I have found comfort of any kind. Now I am advised by others to try on my release to forget that I have ever been in prison at all. I know that would be equally fatal. It would mean that I would always be haunted by an intolerable sense of disgrace, and that those things that are meant for me as much as for anybody else—the beauty of the sun and moon, the pageant of the seasons, the music of daybreak and the silence of great nights, the rain falling through the leaves, or the dew creeping over the grass and making it silver—would all be tainted for me, and lose their healing power and their power of communicating joy. . . . .

I remember talking once on this subject to one of the most beautiful personalities I have ever known: a woman, whose sympathy and noble kindness to me, both before and since the tragedy of my imprisonment, have been beyond power and description; one who has really assisted me, though she does not know it, to bear the burden of my troubles more than anyone else in the whole world has, and all through the mere fact of her existence, through her being what she is—partly an ideal and partly an influence: a suggestion of what one might become as well as a real help toward becoming it; a soul that renders the common air sweet, and makes what is spiritual seem as simple and natural as sunlight or the sea: one for whom beauty and sorrow walk hand in hand, and have the same message. On the occasion of which I am thinking I recall distinctly how I said to her that there was enough *suffering* in one narrow London lane to show that God did not love man, and that wherever there was any sorrow, though but that of a child in some little garden weeping over a fault that it had or had not committed, the whole face of creation was completely marred. I was entirely wrong. She told me so, but I could not believe her. I was not in the sphere in which such belief was to be attained to. Now it seems to me that love of some kind is the only possible explanation of the extraordinary amount of suffering that there is in the world. I cannot conceive of any other explanation. I am convinced that there is no other, and that if the world has indeed, as I have said, been built of sorrow, it has been built by the hands of love, because in no other way could the soul of man, for whom the world was made, reach the full stature of its perfection.[4]

These, then—sense preceptions, time-flight, sins, mental quirks, friends, and suffering—are among the agents of realization. They illustrate ways in which many factors in life experience may bring persons to themselves, to awareness of who and what and where they are, and to a deeper appreciation of the meanings hidden beneath the surfaces of their facts of life. But—realization is not all.

INNER CHANGES ACCOMPANY REALIZATION

Repentance, acknowledgment, and confession. Early among the inner changes that come with realization is repentance. This is a wholly natural process if realization has gone deep in a person still emotionally honest and sensitive to his own standards of rectitude, to the welfare of others, and to the laws of Eternal Rightness. Repentance comes almost of itself when such a person realizes his wrongness. He turns from it quickly to acknowledgment, confession, and rightness. But

[4] Oscar Wilde, *De Profundis.* By permission of G. P. Putnam's Sons.

he whose inner life is hardened by long transgression may realize his wrongness only to find emotional blockages that estop all action. Then inner tragedy ensues. His is a soul at war within. Those who have no sense of Eternal Rightness settle the issue as best they may. To the Christian mind there are always two parties to such an issue: the self—this living, thinking being that dwells within my house of life—and the Eternal Light that lighteth every man coming into the world. This individual "I am" and the vast "I am"—these two are always involved. "Closer is He than breathing, nearer than hands and feet." Directly or indirectly also there is always some third person present. Often there are many other persons and still others beyond others in concentric circles. But repentance for sins must begin with first person I, with acknowledgment by the self to the self. No priest or witness or notary public need be present for that acknowledgment. Ritual confessions to God without profound acknowledgment to the self by the self are meaningless words and may, indeed, become makers of hard-shelled hypocrisy. Self is a wily fellow, evasive, fugitive, very difficult to catch. He, himself, must finally bring himself to stand straight up alone and say to himself, "These are the facts—my facts. These facts make me what I am. I am sorry. These things ought not so to be. They shall not be so again."

"These facts will color all my life, but I am going to choose the color." Those words were spoken out of one man's painful realization of wrongdoing at a crucial moment of choice. Change was possible to him. He could and would make that change by choice. Furthermore, he would make it upward and outward. The very flavor of his words conveys the direction of his spirit. The byways downward were open to him of course—to deny the facts, to throw dust in the air, to blame others, to seek reprisals, to hate and to fight, regardless of consequences to self or others. Or another route was open—

silent refusal to admit anything even to himself, withdrawal, morbid introspection, self-blame, inner dissolution and despair. But this man? Not he! "I admit the facts. I realize their meaning. I have been wrong. I am sorry. I pray for forgiveness. God helping me, I will shape the meaning of this experience to the good of others and myself." Such a choice, like faith in God, is a basic moral choice.

Acknowledgment to self is inseparable from acknowledgment to God. God is so near as Jesus thought of Him that He overhears the first acknowledgment, and that makes the one to Him not difficult. For God by His very nature is an answerer of perplexities, a mender of divided souls and broken relationships who cares about persons with the yearning of Eternal Love. He always keeps open many pathways to Himself. "The Father seeketh such to worship Him."

And so the acknowledgment to other persons is easier than it would be had the first and second not been made. Yet it is often not easy. It is, in fact, in many instances extremely difficult; for dangerous bypaths open again. Shame, pride, and bitterness beckon. But just then one hears, like a warning whispered in the night,

> No, that's the world's way: (keep the mountain-side,
>   Make for the city!)[5]

"Confess to others this evil which I have done? Yes, for I now see many others who have washed their garments white by clean confession, who dwell in a celestial city with peaceful faces and with singing hearts." Confession comes, thus, with acknowledgment and as an integral part of it once the basic choice is made. The sequence is a unitary experience: realization, repentance, acknowledgment, and confession.

Acceptance of unalterable facts as unalterable. When clari-

---

[5] Robert Browning, "A Grammarian's Funeral."

fication comes, when the inner man is purged, the mind is freed, the spirit is liberated, the inner forces are released. All is now clear save for one acceptance yet to be achieved. There are some facts that do not change, acknowledged or unacknowledged. Some consequences, physical, mental, and moral, hang on relentlessly and cannot be altered by any known powers of God or man within the conditions of this mortal life as we now know them. Such unalterability is itself an inescapable fact of human experience. As long as disease and death are still among the given factors in that experience, soon or late they come, as to all men they must. To accept these unavoidable elements in experience, when they arrive, is as necessary as their coming is inevitable. The unalterable can be accepted even though it cannot be altered. There are few more pungent bits anywhere in literature than Margaret Fuller's saying to Carlyle, "I accept the Universe," and Carlyle's remarking aside, "Gad, she'd better."

What, then, is the unalterable? It has two aspects, one related to past experiences, and the other related to the limitations of life at any point of time and circumstance.

First there are such stark unalterable elements in everyone's life as the loss of loved ones. The spiritual acceptance of such facts becomes a crucial issue. We turn again to *De Profundis:*

It is man's soul that Christ is always looking for. He calls it "God's Kingdom," and finds it in everyone. He compares it to little things, to a tiny seed, to a handful of leaven, to a pearl. That is because one *realizes* one's soul only by getting rid of all alien passions, all acquired culture, and all external possessions, be they good or evil.

I bore up against everything with some stubbornness of will and much rebellion of nature, till I had absolutely nothing left in the world but one thing. I had lost my name, my position, my happiness, my freedom, my wealth. I was a prisoner and a pauper. But I still had my children left. Suddenly they were taken away from me by the law. It was a blow so appalling that I did not know what to do, so I flung myself on my knees, and bowed my head, and wept, and said, "The body of a child is as the body of the Lord: I am not worthy of either." That moment seemed to save me. I saw then that the only thing for me was *to accept everything*. Since then—curious as it will no doubt sound—I have been happier. It was of course my soul in its ultimate essence that I had reached. In many ways I had been its enemy, but I found it waiting for me as a friend. When one comes in contact with the soul it makes one simple as a child, as Christ said one should be.

It is tragic how few people ever "possess their souls" before they die. . . . .

He who is in a state of rebellion cannot receive grace, to use the phrase of which the Church is so fond—so rightly fond, I dare say—for in life as in art the mood of rebellion closes up the channels of the soul, and shuts out the airs of heaven. Yet I must learn these lessons here, if I am to learn them anywhere, and must be filled with joy if my feet are on the right road and my face set towards "the gate which is called beautiful," though I may fall many times in the mire and often in the mist go astray.[6]

Victorious acceptance of the unalterable is possible in one's own experience. It is something very different from self-pitying resignation. Such acceptance says with Lanier:

> Old Past, let go, and drop i' the sea
> Till fathomless waters cover thee!
> For I am living but thou art dead;
> Thou drawest back, I strive ahead
> The Day to find.[7]

There are other elements that at any particular moment seem unalterable—and are so for the time being. But they are not to be accepted as permanently so. Science and faith

[6] Oscar Wilde, *De Profundis*. By permission of G. P. Putnam's Sons.
[7] Sidney Lanier, "Barnacles." By permission of Charles Scribner's Sons.

both play their parts in altering them. The science of skillful surgeons illustrates this type excellently. They locate the unalterable at no fixed point. Surgical discoveries make a life continuance today out of the inevitable death of yesterday. Arterial surgery is a sufficiently new and unbelievable discovery to illustrate. The unalterable has been altered by it. Faith shared and permeated the process of that discovery. Faith is not some detached concept apart from living processes of discovery; faith is confidence in the discoverability of new knowledge, in the reliability of the universe, in the recuperative powers of persons, in surgeons and nurses, and in the ultimate forces which, as Jesus believed, are essentially like those we recognize in the finest, ablest persons we know. No one can, therefore, define the precise and permanent limits of the apparently inevitable and unalterable. The issue must be settled in the particular instance, under particular conditions of time and place, and on the basis of the knowledge and powers then and there available. And faith must be continuously applied to the enlargement of such knowledge and power.

Altering alterable facts. There is a moment in the meditative phase of the spiral arc of growth when backward-looking reflection turns toward the future, when retrospect gives way to prospect. "When he came to himself, he said . . . . I will arise and go." Acceptance has a futuristic aspect which becomes a quickener of courage and hope. New insights and impulses come as surely as the march of time—insights which point the way, impulses to pursue that way. "Here is a thing I could change. This I could alter, and that, and that, and that." Not much they seem, perhaps, when first they shyly show their faces. But the whole of a wholesome future hangs on their being welcomed by the backward-looking self and made the most of for the future. There are other impulses also, stronger and more emotionally charged, that sometimes erupt with terrific force, dangerously, like an oil well "coming in."

There are, in fact, two sorts of dangers from impulses, weak and strong. The first danger is that the impulse be so slight, so unaccompanied by emotional discharge that it may be smothered and lost underground, trickling away into the subsoil, moving into subsurface collections of discouragement and unhealthy fixation on unalterable elements in the past. Such impulses need a strengthening nurture. The other danger is that pent-up forces, erupting like a "gusher," will blow oil all over the area and wild, wasteful, or dangerous action result. This kind of impulsiveness needs control. The gusher must be capped, the flow channeled, and reservoirs built to regularize its distribution.

Both types of impulses need preparation for social use. Socially useful expression is their true end. Such expression necessitates meditative preparation. Some of that preparation comes about by deep and secret forces flowing into consciousness from insights, inner illuminations, guidances, the voice of the Eternal (call them as we each prefer), and in part by conscious preparation and inner commitments. These come in delicate moments of inner experience that defy description. They are like the split second of curving pause when rising water-drops turn over to the falling, or when the late night twilight brightens into the red light of dawn. So, when inner impulses deliver themselves over to conscious use, an exquisitely potential moment has come. The rightness of future action depends upon the meditative quiet of that moment, its protection from outer blighting and from inner haste. These words reveal such a moment. "I see now where I was wrong. There are changes I can make. I will make them. I understand wherein I failed. I will not fail at that point again."

"I have been petty, small, and mean-spirited. I see it now.

I see now what I have been doing to my colleagues on the faculty—how my own spirit has been shriveling for a year, while I was bitter and blaming them. I now commit myself to generous judgments of them, and most of all of the two persons in our department who, for some strange reason, have been most irritating to me. They will find me understanding and co-operative from this day on."

"I had not realized how my obstinacy in what I thought was a justifiable policy is blighting this whole company where I hold the control of the stock. I did not realize that my self-ishness meant such terrible poverty and disease for those women and children of our workers whom we saw today. Now I recognize my responsibility. I shall change those policies. I shall cut that demand I've made of the managers for a straight profit of twenty per cent to me. I shall cut it to six per cent at most, and put the difference into the pay envelopes of our people. There are living conditions I can change—housing conditions, prices of food, and hours of labor. These are under my control. I commit myself to their change. I see it now. I see it all. There are a thousand things that I can change—things in myself, in my attitudes, my very ways of speaking to people, my methods of dealing with them. Pretty much all my relationships with people need changing. I will change them. There are great things I could do with these resources of mine to help our helpers. I will do them."

Acceptance of fellow workers. Did you notice how the ego bulked large in that last section? It easily does so with people in positions of power—even among the saints, especially among some of the prominent saints such as leaders of so-called movements, pulpit orators, bishops, and dictators, feminine as well as masculine. Let them now lead us humbly to another form of realization and acceptance which reduces the ego to the ranks, magnifies God and the common people.

REALIZING THE MEANINGS OF FACTS

The pronounced egocentrics among the saints, who are really relying on the power of their official positions for social control, sometimes make us wonder why their personal relationships are not more creative. Their reliance upon their status is probably the reason. For whenever church officials or other holders of public office do not admit the Eternal and the common workers into fully-shared partnership of responsibility and credit, they tend to move toward the militaristic opposite of the Spirit of Jesus.

The acceptance of the humblest workers to full participation is implicit in the democratic process, implicit in all Christian teaching. He said, "I am in the midst of you as he that serveth. . . . . Ye know that the rulers of the Gentiles lord it over them, and their great ones exercise authority over them. Not so shall it be among you: but whosoever would become great among you shall be your minister; and whosoever would be first among you shall be your servant: even as the Son of man came not be ministered unto, but to minister, and to give his life a ransom for many."

Men who learn how to work humbly with the universe, its laws and its forces, also learn how to let the universe work in and through them. That is to "accept the universe" in another sense. That acceptance is in the mood of Jesus. So profoundly are men imbedded in cosmic forces, and so mysteriously creative are those forces within them, that he who commits his life to creative relationships lives, moves, and has his being, according to Jesus, in eternal and universal love, the greatest of all forces. For all prominent persons thus to see themselves in the view of eternity results in a desirable kind of humility which manifestly could be of benefit in all aspects of American life by a deeper psychological penetration.

The Eternal and the common workers—they are the really important persons. To accept them both completely into the inner circle of a wholly shared life is creative acceptance indeed.

JESUS DEEPENS THE REALIZATION OF MEANINGS

Always above and on beyond His disciples in His grasp of spiritual meanings, Jesus is none the less realistic. He seems always to have been getting and appraising the practical facts in actual life situations—as of those persons, for example, who built on sand instead of on rock, those who built or did not build counting the costs in advance, those who did or did not load other men with burdens grievous to be borne. The parables all show His thinking as intensely practical, concrete, and realistic.

Jesus deepens likewise the realization of the meaning of persons themselves. What do you think was Jesus' most profound realization about persons as He moved among them, knew them, and loved them? If we could find the answer to that question, we might find the clue to His all-embracing thought about man and God. That might lead us to the indispensable element in creative relationships.

We pick up the clue in modern France from the beautiful French word *sacré*. In a Roman Catholic church in Trouville one kneels near a war mother praying before a tablet inscribed to Jacques and Henri. Their memory is a sacred memory because they themselves were sacred. The place is sacred because of them—French boys who said with their lives at Verdun, "Ye shall not pass." Others like them now gone but not forgotten sanctify this place. Therefore the incense burns. Therefore men and women come hither to pray. This historic church, like innumerable other churches, is sacred, above all, because of Jesus. His life and death have made them so. Persons sanctify places before places in due season deepen awareness of the sanctity of persons. This, one comes to understand, is Jesus' deepest realization about persons. They are inherently sacred, not flesh alone, but spirit also—all *sacré*. Gratitude to thee, Jacques. Gratitude to thee, Henri. Gratitude to thee, sorrowing mother. Gratitude to Thee, Jesus, for this moment of fresh realization that human life is eternally *sacré*.

That concept, we dare to say, is the most anti-pagan, anti-secular concept ever brought to clarify the realizations of men and women about personality. A person is indescribably valuable, as if he were a king's son, crown prince of the realm. Others have held similar concepts too: one person sacred enough to serve as emperor, object of worship, untouchably sacred, however ignorant or cruel; a few persons held sacred and superior to all common persons, like vestal virgins or consecrated priests or an oligarchy of wealth, of warrior courage, scholarship, or ethical rectitude. All these concepts have been tried again and again in history, but all have missed *His* mark. Not one alone, not a few, not a superior class or oligarchy, but *all* persons—that is the paradox He brings. All men, women and children—everyone is *sacré*. Even the most repulsive of persons, demoniac men, epileptics, and loathsome lepers—there are none outside His circle. None of the shamed or scorned, the ugly or crippled, the vicious or criminal are without the temple gates. Everyone is within His "Whosoever." That constitutes the uniqueness of His realization about persons. That is His distinguishing great idea. That is the most revolutionary concept ever flung in the face of the animalism of the barbarian world, the cold superiority of Greece, the ruthless cruelty of Rome. That, with its companionate concepts of restoration, nurture, and potential perfection, imparts its quality to that Realm of God which is both human and divine—the Realm that is and is to be.

So Jesus, implanting this great truth in persons, is the supreme agent of realization in the life of the world.

A PERSON-MINDED MINISTRY

Perplexed people are asking everywhere, "Who, what, and where am I? are we?"

Jesus answers: "You are a child of the Eternal, and your life is sacred. You are what you are—what your own facts say you are. You are in your Father's house, where there are many abiding places, where there is both room and welcome for all."

What, then, do His ministers most need in America and everywhere? What else so much as deep realizations, complete acceptances? In quiet hours of meditation, in between the hours of action, they need to find the "returning and the rest" in which they shall be saved.

> Oh, save me from the haste and noise and heat
> That spoil life's music sweet.[8]

[8] Edward Rowland Sill, "The Venus de Milo."

V

ACTING ON THE BASIS OF FACTS

OUR fourth essential, stressing rightness in action, follows naturally. It hatches out as a lively bird in the quiet nest of meditation. Eruptive insights follow fact-getting, fact-facing, realization, and acceptance. Healthy-minded realization naturally breaks out with a program and demonstrates by renewed action the rhythmic development of experience.

"When he came to himself, he said . . . . I will arise and go."

"And he arose, and came."

The negative pick-up points are in human lethargy and perversity. Despite man's being by nature an activist animal, quick on his feet, highly muscular, and of nimble wit, many persons are characterized by lethargy. "Plain lazy" is the usual description. There are, however, other causes than the native inertia to which lethargy is ordinarily ascribed. Among these are debilitating heat and humidity in southern latitudes, racial inheritances and low orders of culture, insufficient stimulus to effective labor, lack of practical training in general education, energy-sapping diseases such as hookworm, malaria, pellagra, and venereals, debilitating excesses in sex, in drinking, and eating. Another group of causes has come out of man's inhumanity to man; the cruelties of slavery, peonage, and other labor exploitations, inadequate supplies of nourishing food and shelter, and indecent, unsanitary living and working conditions. Any student of human lethargy has several sets of facts to assemble and realize before he accepts the superficial interpretation of "born laziness." Personal inertia of our own leads most of us to a suitable state of humility in this respect, but when inertia is viewed as an aspect of social pathology, social causes become increasingly apparent.

It is much the same with widely accepted ideas about man's so-called "natural perversity," "innate cussedness," "total depravity," as if there were a crooked grain in the native stock. Another convenient interpretation imputes responsibility for evil to an omnipresent devil—fallen angel or descendant of animistic sprites. Responsibility has also been imputed to God as the Creator of all things, so that there might be a reputable hell from which men could be rescued, and to overt choice of evil by Adam or others. Such interpretations have been, for the most part, sincere efforts to get at some aspect of wrongness in human life and account for it, but one important element has been omitted from practically all of them. That is the element of social causation.

During maltreated childhood much stubborn negativism comes into consciousness. In the selfishness and deceit within many families and between rival groups much resentment is born. Out of injustices committed by land-grabbers and other hogs of natural resources, long-lasting enmities have developed. Out of profit-seeking extortion in business deep hostility against the social system has been engendered. Ignorance of natural laws has led to bitterness against the universe. The horrors of war have given rise to despair and to wickednesses worse than those of savagery. Out of man's overt choice of evil ways with weaker persons such as women and children has come a sense of guilt which he seeks to escape by projecting it upon society and the universe. Therefore the student of human behavior will not accept any superficial interpretation of human perversity, but will study social as well as personal causes with care. "Natural perversity," as most of us

92

know on a certain amount of internal evidence, accounts for some of it, but certainly not all. Social causes bulk large.

NATURAL IMPULSIVENESS AND HUNGER FOR RIGHTNESS

The improved action which normally follows realistic meditation is based upon the opposites of lethargy and perverseness, upon native energy and upon natural desires for rightness in life and relationships. To these, then, we turn. The native energy which impregnates action is not to be undervalued. Impulses to right action break through in the quiet of meditative hours and set persons forward by their eruptive power. By these, unless they are blocked, men are enabled to do the things they should. Meditate for a moment, then, upon the gift of human energy. Mysterious as a living spring flowing clear in the depths of the forest, as the surge of the tide on an ocean shore, native human energy expresses itself in play and work, in the merry shouts of boys and girls, in flashing eyes and romping games, in the steady labor of maturer years, in aged "eyes undimmed," and in natural forces unabated. It results from food, sleep, and exercise and a thousand chemical, physical, spiritual adjustments. Mysterious and priceless, it impregnates all life with zest. Let those who for any reason lack it testify.

Whence came all the medieval antipathy to natural impulsiveness? Why this morbid fear of natural desires? There is no natural human impulse which does not have legitimate time, place, companionship, and setting for its exercise. Gratitude to the sun-bright source of eternal energy is the wholesome attitude in regard to natural impulses rather than fear or suppression of them. In native energy clean honesty is found. In it creative relationships find their physical source of creativity. It shows at its lively best in the spontaneous activities of healthy children, in their questioning interest in all life offers them, in the winged flights of their imagination, and in the shy outreaches of their eager spirits. So natural human energy is to be validated in our thought and utilized for high ends in personal growth and relationships. Spontaneity is to be aided and empowered in its persistent warfare against drab lethargy, the sag of life toward ennui, and the paralysis of man's best powers. Normal, healthy men and women, lovers of work and play, rightly rejoice in the resilient energies that leap in their arteries, flex their muscles, quicken their minds, and swing them out in lively adventures. When God set native human energy afoot, He must have said, "That's good."

There is full reason, likewise, to stress the native rightness that is in persons, in their impulses to self-improvement, to fair play, social justice, and abundance of life. There is much greater reason indeed to stress these than man's mistakes or overt choices of evil. A strain of morbidity runs through much so-called religious literature and preaching, which puts a disproportionate emphasis upon sin without any adequate recognition of man's native hunger for rightness. The result is a distorted picture. On the other hand, emphasis upon every impulse to rightness increases rightness just as blood flows faster at the sound of quickening music. Away, then, with all morbid fixation on the sins and shortcomings of the past, when once honest facing, realizing, and confessing have taken place. Morbid dwelling upon sins already confessed and abandoned has wrought havoc in many a person. The facts that bring out native rightness have equal right, yes, better right to recognition, review, and emphasis. Great gratitude is in order for works wrought by man's native love of beauty and goodness.

This native hunger for rightness shows itself in the eager wholesomeness of children, in the hunger of young people for education, in their willingness to co-operate, in their demands for social justice, and in their spontaneous generosities in the face of so much greed and selfishness. We stand in wondering awe before the volume of the love of goodness, beauty, and the truth there is in men and women, and especially in children. In view of their ancestry, and in light of all the evil and brutality that have been foisted upon them, it is amazing to find in men, women, and children so much inherent rightness.

This basis of approach to persons is far from the shallow optimism which is often imputed to it. Rather, it leads one deep into the tragedy of human experience and makes vividly real the perversion, exploitation, and corruption of young life, of weak persons and defenseless groups, wherever these occur. It brings one sharply to realize one's own participation in social injustices and makes one humbly grateful for the evil-resistant powers of man. He must belong to God rather than to evil, else he would have gone down utterly eons ago. When God made man He made him in His own image, and when He set man's native love of rightness afoot, He must have said, "That's good."

With gratitude, then, for all natural impulses and all native rightness in persons we turn to the rectification of past errors and overt wrongness. Rectifications are needed for clarification of spirit and for the sake of justice to others. It is evident that these two processes are necessary for the unification of personality, for the restoration and enrichment of relationships between persons, for the establishment of justice in the earth, and for rightness in relationships with the Eternal.

JESUS STRESSES RIGHTNESS IN RELATIONSHIPS

What, then, do we find is the heart of Jesus' teaching with regard to rightness in life and power to achieve that rightness? He grew up in the midst of the well-established Jewish system of negative regulations, minutely calculated to enforce rightness. Jesus, however, does not use the method of *pro-*

scription as do the makers of laws and ordinances, *pro*scribing all manner of major and minor offenses, crimes, and misdemeanors and assigning penalties on the basis of things done, rather than the culpability of the persons doing them. Nor does Jesus put His reliance upon the *pre*scription of detailed requirements—a *pre*scribed set of duties outlined in advance for all conceivable circumstances and relationships. His method is not to formalize life and ethics on rigid patterns. Formalization of conduct occurs when detailed prescriptions are conformed to, while hypocrisy and guilt-consciousness characterize those who do not conform.

So, also, the method of isolating and abstracting certain so-called virtues, such as sincerity, patience, and the like, Jesus avoids. His method is not to catalogue the virtues one by one, as pedantic minds have done, thereby robbing them of the charm they have when embodied in persons. To catalogue the virtues makes them into a mere ethical index to the book of life. Nor did Jesus create a set of maxims like the Book of Proverbs saying, for example, as He might well have done, "Better is a dinner of herbs where love is, than a stalled ox and hatred therewith." Even the so-called Sermon on the Mount is a collection of His utterances evidently spoken on various occasions, with reference to the specific needs of particular persons. The systematization of principles was not His method.

Rather does He see and describe living persons, whole persons, with their predominant wrongnesses and rightnesses. Who can forget the persons He describes: the wise and foolish virgins, the man whose barns were bursting with crops, the prodigal's elder brother who was angry and would not rejoice with the rest of the family, the woman who lost her money and found it, the man who found the precious pearl, the bride and the bridegroom, and many another! He teaches always about persons in relationships, especially the human-divine relationship. He is therefore always clarify-

ing what He means by quality in a life. Over and over again
He illustrates or implies what he means by the fineness of the
finest persons, the finest relationships, the finest society—all
illustrating the quality of the Eternal Person Himself. That
is His emphasis, and He relentlessly contrasts it to the rule-
made righteousness of the scribes and Pharisees.

The quality of eternal rightness was His quest. He sought
it everywhere in ordinary persons. He spoke with them about
it and illustrated it with imperishable stories when He talked
with little groups. His own exquisite fineness and strength
personified it, for He achieved it in Himself. He relied upon
it in the Heart of the Universe when He passed through incalculable suffering in the might of it. He triumphed over
death and apparent defeat, trusting in the rightness that is eternal. That is why men who realize even a little of His power
want to turn from wrongness in His presence and seek the
rightness of His quality of life.

To all men who join His quest of rightness Jesus brings
the power to achieve it. The reality of that power endures.
He knew full well the disillusionment of those whose ideals
are unaccompanied by power to achieve them. Whenever
men and women assemble, face, and realize their own facts,
they intuitively sense their need for power greater than their
own to help them achieve visions of what they want to be
and do.

> I feel me near to some High Thing
>   That earth awaits from me,
> But cannot tell in all my journeying
>   What it may be.[1]

He tells men what *it* is. He gives them power both to find
it and to achieve it in ends that are worthy of the God-given

[1] William Ellery Leonard, "I feel me near to some High Thing," from *The
Vaunt of Man*. Copyright 1912. By permission of The Viking Press, Inc.,
New York.

dignity of persons and their best aspirations. So those who see Him clearly turn naturally to him for His unexampled understanding of persons with all their divine possibilities and for that mysterious communicable energy which He conveys. He vitalizes their aspirations and enables them to weld ideals into deeds. To those who humbly seek to realize His rightness in themselves and to establish it in society He imparts the living energy they need to rectify their lives and to share it creatively with others. What a cloud of witnesses testify to that! He brings deep healing and new power. He releases creativity.

So utterly did He trust Eternal Energy and Eternal Rightness in righted persons that He calmly said to His disciples, "The works that I do shall ye do also; and greater works than these shall ye do."

There is one way for thee; but one; inform thyself of it; pursue
it; one way each
Soul hath by which the infinite in reach
Lieth before him; seek and ye shall find.[2]

"Attempt great things for God; expect great things from God."

RECTIFYING PAST MISTAKES AND DELINQUENCIES

The heritage of wrongness. Wrongness of some sort in individuals has always been recognized in Christian thought. The concept of sin goes far back into Hebrew history as offense against the Holy One and His laws. The fact of sin in the sense of breaking established laws or customs is older still. Its origins are lost in primitive jungles with primitive men. Wherever a standard of rectitude of any sort appeared, there also infractions of that standard appeared. The long black story of ruthless selfishness and of overt choice of

[2] Richard Watson Dixon, "The One Way."

evil, of sin in the hearts and lives of men, has had a rightful emphasis in Jewish-Christian thinking. But in recent years there has come a deeper understanding of sin and a surer knowledge of certain causes of it. The social and mental maladjustments which often lie back of conscious or unconscious evil are seen in truer perspective. This knowledge increases our understanding of human tragedy. Clinical psychology has made great contributions at this point. There has also come a far deeper realization of the social causes of evil, the powerfully established injustices in modern society as a whole. The approaches which had been for centuries chiefly theological and philosophical have now been supplemented, deepened, and at points corrected by searching studies of socially intrenched evils, by studies in social psychology and especially social pathology with its double presentation of personal demoralization and social disorganization.

Realistic minds do not ignore the enormous wrongnesses in American life: the prevalence of vice and crime, poverty, ill health, suffering and unemployment, the inequitable distribution of wealth, the disproportionate rewards of human labor, the exploitation of women and children and of weaker races. Nor can they ignore the prevalence of bitter hostilities in our common life, whether temporarily suppressed or flaming out in strikes and racial hostilities. There is a heritage of devastating wrongness in all the major areas of human relationship which is passed on to successive generations both in American life and in the world life. This is now realized more widely and deeply than ever before. The facts are well in hand, assembled, classified, and vividly presented, thanks to many scientifically-minded workers. Clearly the time for action has arrived.

Intelligent rectifications must be made. There are no escapes. Changes for the better must be brought about. More intelligent actions than ever before must be taken, else down the scale we go again toward bitter hatred and sadistic persecutions, toward systematized slaughter of innocents and ruthless war. Wherein are we in America so different from other peoples who have but lately gone slipping down that road? Are we? The actions to be taken must be intelligent right actions, just as they must be in bodily surgery. The issues are tight issues of life and death for vast numbers of persons. There must be no needless bloodletting on top of all the sufferings already endured.

Human efforts to right the wrongnesses in relationships embrace a multitude of programs. Some are fanciful panaceas; some are tested by time and prove themselves effective. There are always persons with so-called "dangerous" ideas as to what should be done in any democracy. But they and we are better off with them at large than in concentration camps or jails. They must be fairly heard and their ideas judged by their fellows. Sharp discrimination of their ideas is, in fact, a civic duty. These might prove to be constructive even though unfamiliar. Experimental testing and practical social judgments are indispensable in a democracy. Persons who work in the mood of Jesus do not rightly include the shallow optimists, the conservative pessimists, the "do-nothings," or those who deny the reality of evil. We find no answers among the escapists, some of whom move to an otherworldliness that evades all social issues, while others drop into supposedly bomb-proof cellars of self-interest and financial security. Others run away to monasteries and nunneries, social, psychological, and religious. Some side-slide into mere verbalization about what ought to be done. Others retreat into esoteric groups in scholarship and esthetics. Such groups turn unseeing eyes toward the tragic needs in the common life. Some even join the army or the navy to escape. But there are no escapes, and the short-cuts do not really cut through.

Yet there are answers in the mood of Jesus. They have to

be worked out in courageous intelligent action in every area and on all fronts. Solutions, both personal and social, in a world of persons always begin with one person. That person is a self. Solutions begin with honest acknowledgment to the self, to the Eternal, and to injured persons, of wrongness for which one is oneself responsible. When forthright acknowledgment and confession are made by persons the tides of being in themselves and others turn and move toward the future. But they do not so move unless such basic actions are taken by individuals, by groups, and by societies. Truly creative action admits no half measures, no substitutes.

Rectifying action begins with inner changes. Forgiveness has to be given, bitterness has to be stopped, and restitution accepted. Suppose we begin with the sense of being aggrieved, unjustly treated, "put upon," and persecuted. Self-pity, twin sister of the trick of blaming others, is one of the most prevalent and persistent of all states of mind in persons. Self-pity increases rapidly whenever initiative and freedom to act pass from the self to others, from individuals to public agencies, and the sense of personal potentiality is thereby cut down. Actual wrongs and injustices are in need of being forgiven just as much as imagined ones, for the real injustices more surely mar creative relationships. Even persecutions and revilings come in for forgiveness, according to Jesus. When the offending party comes to realization, stops his offenses, makes all possible restitution, and asks forgiveness, is forgiveness fully granted? Is restitution sincerely accepted? Is the spirit of the wronged one cleared of bitterness and his psychological slate washed clean by such acceptances? Refusal to forgive and to accept the proffered restitution is a sure way to deepen bitterness of soul. A new bitterness enters in. The spirit is then reinfected and more deeply poisoned than before. Readiness to forgive must not merely stand waiting at the gate to welcome advances from others. More is required. He who forgives must go a mile outside the gate, yes, a second mile, advancing with a flag of truce and with signs of readiness to close the breach visible in every gesture of his behavior. Furthermore, he must keep on going out into no-man's land expectantly seventy times seven times. This does not mean four hundred and ninety times; it means indefinitely, continuously, till the hardness of the other breaks down from within and he asks to be forgiven. No less difficult action than this is implied in Jesus' teaching and example: "Father, forgive them (I have forgiven them), for they know not what they do."

Rectification also depends upon seeking forgiveness. To stop the wrongdoing and to make restitution are equally essential. Strangely enough, few broken relationships are due to the faults of one person or of one group alone! Who is there who, in the quiet hours of fact-facing, does not come to realization that he also is a "miserable offender?" If such realization has not come to a man, then he had better think through the sources of his financial income, his labor relations, his toleration of political corruption in his own party, his silent acquiescence in economic injustices and the war system, his attitudes toward persons of other races or toward repellent persons and those who are particularly irritating to him among his associates. Incidentally, he might also ask himself if there are any old unconfessed misdemeanors, any old grudges or unresolved hostilities buried beneath the surfaces of his consciousness. If, by that time, he has not come to awareness of any wrongness for which he needs to ask forgiveness, let him think for a time on the achievements of his life as compared with his potentialities and his privileges. If that does not reduce him to some degree of humility and readiness to seek forgiveness for omissions as well as commissions, then he will have proven himself to be a perfect illustration of paranoid delusion.

When realization comes the immediate steps to be taken are to stop all wrong attitudes and actions. To ask forgiveness and to make restitution are inescapable obligations, as Jesus thinks of the matter. They are prerequisites for redeeming the past, for cleansing desires, for restoring relationships, and for getting on with the great business yet to be done. But to ask forgiveness is often most difficult. Shame, pride, self-esteem all rush to the gates to block the outward sally. Yet not to ask forgiveness is to put shame, pride, and self-esteem in possession of the inner life, to habituate that life to an inner duality of high impulse versus low performance. That duality hardens into dividedness of personality and unhealed breaches of relationship. It soon leads downward through another gateway to evasion of responsibility, to increased blaming of others, to insensibility to social injustice, to new offenses, to more and more ruptured relationships, and, perhaps, to ruthless exploitation and overt violence. But he who humbly walks through the narrow gate out into no-man's-land eager to be forgiven, with a flag of truce in one hand and restitution in the other, finds both forgiveness and rectification. By every possible means he seeks to restore to others the stolen values, be they lands, goods, damages to personality, reputation, or honor. Jesus' requirement for rectification, however difficult, is to stop one's wrongdoing, to make restitution, and to ask forgiveness.

Rectification is followed by peace. But the requirements have to be fulfilled. The peace Jesus promised can be had only by paying the price. It is a matter of common experience in social relationships that hostilities tend to die down and bitterness to soften with the flight of time. Truces and quiescence, if not peace, ensue. Forgiveness is a means of hastening this slow process. Forgiveness deals actively, constructively, and creatively. The advent of peace is hastened, and initial peace deepens into permanent peace if the search-

103

ing requirements of forgiveness, restitution, and stoppage of wrongdoing are fulfilled. In every relationship, in every area where these requirements are fulfilled in honest mutuality, peace ensues. Recent history has amply demonstrated the futility of peace talk and peace societies without the fulfillment of these indispensable requirements. To want peace without paying the price for it is symbolic of that spirit in modern men which wants something for nothing, much for little, yet refuses to pay the price that life requires.

Jesus *won* the peace he promised to those who follow Him. "Peace I leave with you; my peace I give unto you: not as the world giveth, give I unto you." No man may know all the elements that entered into the steady poise, the imperturbability of Jesus in those hours of His betrayal, when He was denied, mocked, and scourged by His sadistic persecutors, and finally nailed to the cross, the ultimate symbol of public shame. But surely every person who has needed forgiveness and has been given it, who has needed to forgive and has forgiven, knows the cleansing peace that follows. He has discovered that the peace which Jesus gives his followers has in it always this element of forgiveness. Jesus incarnated all that He taught. His peace awaits all those who achieve mastery over life wherever they are caught in the toils of small or great offenses. Each one may have it freely as bread and wine at sacrament if only he has both asked and given forgiveness.

PROJECTING THE FUTURE

Up and out!

The world lies east: how ample the marsh and the sea and the
    sky! . . . .
Oh, what is abroad in the marsh and the terminal sea?
    Somehow my soul seems suddenly free
From the weighing of fate and the sad discussion of sin

ACTING ON THE BASIS OF FACTS

By the length and the breadth and the sweep of the marshes of
Glynn.[8]

It has taken us a long time to get through the gateway of
forgiveness out into the sunlight of the beckoning future.
Now we are free at last, "breast and back as either should be,"
free "to greet the unseen with a cheer," free to rejoice in whatever future lies before us, and "fit to employ all the heart and
the soul and the senses forever in joy." At long last we have
come to another turning in the spiral arc of growth, to an
action-phase again, which has been clarified by fact-getting
and fact-facing, by meditation and prayer, by realization and
acceptance, by rectification through forgiveness given and
sought. We seek now to do whatever we ought to do, whatever we can still do, and what now—strange as it would have
seemed a while ago—we really want to do. We press on to
such true ends of action as have been clarifying themselves in
each of us throughout these meditations.

Ever forward was the mood of Jesus, never hasting, but
never ceasing to be on about His Father's business. In quality His intensity was at the opposite extreme from American
busyness; yet it carried Him on and on from one village to
another, rectifying and quickening persons, spreading the
glad news of possible rightness, beauty, and truth in all persons, and the great news of Eternal Love always available to
them from the great *I Am*. "Let us go elsewhere into the
next towns that I may interpret there also, for to this end
came I forth." And Jesus went about in all Galilee teaching
in their synagogues and interpreting the glad tidings and
rectifying all kinds of personal wrongness and all kinds of illness among the people. Freely, now, we move in the length
and the breadth and the sweep of the purposes of the Eternal.

[8] Sidney Lanier, "The Marshes of Glynn." By permission of Charles
Scribner's Sons.

A PERSON-MINDED MINISTRY

I needs must hurry with the wind
And trim me best for sailing.[4]

Faith in the future is a natural assumption. More than action itself is involved in any action. The whole of the future
will be shaped and, it may be, altered profoundly by that
which is now done. Every action of persons is potential,
crammed with incalculable meaning for the future. The future beckons to us from the western hilltops, signals to us on
the eastern slopes. Strangely we assume the future; we bank
on it, do business with it, proceed on the basis of it, and plant
bulbs in the fall for April flowering just as if assurance of
life were as surely guaranteed as assurance of death. That in
itself is a happy mental fact. Life assurance is a pleasant
companion to live with, more pleasant far than a death date
or a death phobia. Strange "timebinding" creature man,
possessed of a past, present, and future, sure of the present
only, and none too sure of that! The past seems to be assured (if wars become not too destructive) by reason of
human memory, books, and such vestiges of it as are in human
behavior, human institutions, and other museums of antiquity.
But the future is as sure as the sun and as the stars in their
courses. The future is safeguarded, furthermore, by the
strange and universal gift of imagination, by man's ability
to bind into the present the future which is to be, but which
never yet has been. This he does with an unbelievable sense
of assurance. Paradoxically elusive as the future is, it runs
straight toward us, jumps over our heads in a trice, and hides
away in some nook or cranny of the past before we are aware
of its arrival. Then it shouts to us like a child at hide-and-
go-seek, "If you want me, look for me here." Imagination,
pregnant with past experience, flies all about exploring the

[4] Sidney Lanier, "Barnacles." By permission of Charles Scribners's Sons.

future with the utmost assurance, untroubled by the flight of time.

Among all the sons of men it is the musicians who best understand the art of imagining the future and making it join hands with the past in the present.

And I know not if, save in this, such gift be allowed to man,
   That out of three sounds he frame, not a fourth sound, but a
     star. . . . .
All we have willed or hoped or dreamed of good shall exist;
   Not its semblance, but itself; no beauty, nor good, nor power
Whose voice has gone forth, but each survives for the melodist,
   When eternity affirms the conception of an hour.[5]

Imagination explores the unknown endlessly, not alone with the witchery of music, with fanciful dreams of sprites and fairies, lovely as they may be, not alone with mythologies and day-dreams, revealing as they do the subsurface mental world, but also with mathematical calculations that outleap the speed of cosmic rays to the precise moment when centuries hence an eclipse shall occur. So likewise with its feet on the ground or underground in the bowels of the earth, imagination helps prepare the bids and specifications to build bridges, to excavate mines and tunnels, to make estimates for the risking of millions on the basis of accurate projections into the future. "Got to use your imagination all the time," said a hard-headed contractor. "Got to guess, keep on guessing, and guess right. I had to estimate on thirty jobs last year; had to bid on each one so that I could win if I got the job and yet underbid all the other bidders. I was lucky to get two out of the thirty and I'm going to win on both." Along with this sort of imaginative projection goes a basic and fundamental faith in the reliability of the future. Without imagina-

---

[5] Robert Browning, "Abt Vogler."

tion, based on such faith, there could be no scientific hypotheses, no new construction work, no great discoveries, no art, no creative relationships.

If imagination explores the future, the affirmative mind takes its life in its hand and enters it. "Act now." "Use all your resources." "Go forward." "Nothing risked, nothing gained." "Seek ye the Lord while He may be found. Call ye upon Him while he is near." Never in lethargic dawdling, never in the mulishness of negation, shall the quest be found. By affirmation looking through the eyes of faith is the entry made.

If the affirmative mind takes men and women into the future, it is the spirit of youth that soon outruns them and leads on in the further way. "A little child shall lead them." The children are the future here in visible presence, sitting at our tables, playing all about our dooryards where we go in and out concerned with present urgencies. They call out, "Oh, come and play with us. We know you won't be around here long. You don't quite understand, but you really belong to the past already, now that we have come. So please play with us and answer all our questions. Teach us all the beautiful games you know." Fathers and mothers understand best about this—especially those who no longer have to wash out baby clothes and hang up diapers on the clothesline. But fathers and mothers whose boys and girls have grown up and gone away from home and come back only now and then from college or the job in the city—they understand all about it. They find it a little difficult to speak about, even to their ministers; yet they accept it and say quietly to each other, "Yes, the future belongs to them."

> The world is very old,
> A troop of shadows moving with the sun;
> Thousands of times has the old tale been told.

ACTING ON THE BASIS OF FACTS

The world belongs to those who come the last.
They will find hope and strength as we have done.[6]

The spirit of youth leads on the way.

Intelligent courage welds the future into a stable present and a solid past. It is the faint-hearted who fail. The courageous never fail. The courageous-minded who know how to use their problem-solving brains, who get, face, realize, accept, and utilize all their pertinent facts, in teamwork with men and God—they do not fail. They may go down—oh yes, most men go under for a season, soon or late, else they are never born again out of the past, and out of the present into the future. Some, indeed, have finally to go on out into the great Beyond saying, "On the earth the broken arcs; in the heaven a perfect round." But fail! Not they! They know that often "shall life succeed in that it seems to fail." They learn to

Strive, and hold cheap the strain;
Learn, nor account the pang; dare, never grudge the throe! [7]

Intelligent courage achieves the future. If we rightly assume the future, if imagination explores it, if the affirmative mind enters it, if the spirit of youth leads on the way within it, then courage will achieve it and cannot fail. To achieve the future is to make a success of the past, for, at last, the past is "all that there is."

Faith is indispensable in achieving the ends of Jesus. It makes all the difference in the world when His ends are the ones actually accepted and worked for by any person or group of persons. Faith is no abstract virtue to be hunted up under letter F in a theological index. It is a living quality in the lives of living persons.

[6] Henry Wadsworth Longfellow, "A Shadow."
[7] Robert Browning, "Rabbi Ben Ezra."

"He whom I accept as righteous will find life through his faith. But if a man draws back, my heart can take no pleasure in him."

But we will not draw back and perish, but we will have faith and save our souls.

Faith means the assurance of what we hope for; it is our conviction about things that we cannot see. For it was by it that the men of old gained God's approval.[8]

Who does not need to read and reread that epic of faith in Hebrews, chapters ten to twelve, which recounts the triumphs of those whose "aspirations are for a better, a heavenly country . . . . who by their faith conquered kingdoms, attained uprightness, received new promises, shut the mouths of lions, put out furious fires, escaped death by the sword, found strength in their time of weakness, proved mighty in war, put foreign armies to flight. Women had their dead restored to them by resurrection. Others endured torture and refused to accept release, that they might rise again to the better life. Still others had to endure taunts and blows, and even fetters and prison. They were stoned to death, they were tortured to death, they were sawed in two, they were killed with the sword. Clothed in the skins of sheep or goats, they were driven from place to place, destitute, persecuted, misused —men of whom the world was not worthy—wandering in deserts, mountains, caves, and holes in the ground."

What a heritage! "So tighten your loosening hold! Stiffen your wavering stand!"

Well may the righted live by faith. The righted have incalculable resources to draw upon. The Eternal God is with them—"our Lord Immanuel." Over and over again Christian persons are reminded that they are never alone. They are always in a fellowship group however isolated they may seem

[8] Hebrews 10:38—11:2. Goodspeed translation.

for the moment to be. They are in a fellowship group whose resources are set deep in the very structures of the universe, in the Eternal Source and Ground of All. The divine companionship is ever present. "I the Lord am with thee." From cover to cover the Sourcebook of Christianity throbs with that great message to living persons. Isaiah is full of it:

Hast thou not known? hast thou not heard? The everlasting God, Jehovah, the Creator of the ends of the earth, fainteth not, neither is weary; there is no searching of his understanding. He giveth power to the faint; and to him that hath no might he increaseth strength. Even the youths shall faint and be weary, and the young men shall utterly fall: but they that wait for Jehovah shall renew their strength; they shall mount up with wings as eagles; they shall run, and not be weary; they shall walk, and not faint.[9]

The Psalms are full of it:

> He that hath clean hands, and a pure heart;
> Who hath not lifted up his soul unto falsehood,
> And hath not sworn deceitfully.
> He shall receive a blessing from Jehovah,
> And righteousness from the God of his salvation.[10]

> Jehovah is my shepherd, I shall not want.[11]

> Jehovah is my light and my salvation;
> Whom shall I fear?
> Jehovah is the strength of my life;
> Of whom shall I be afraid? [12]

Both the consciousness and the messages of Jesus are full of it:

[9] Isaiah 40:28-31.
[10] Psalm 24:4,5.
[11] Psalm 23:1.
[12] Psalm 27:1.

I have told you this while I am still staying with you, but the Helper, the holy Spirit which the Father will send in my place, will teach you everything and remind you of everything that I have told you.[13]

St. Paul is full of it:

He hath said unto me, My grace is sufficient for thee: for my power is made perfect in weakness.[14]

Yea verily, and I count all things to be loss for the excellency of the knowledge of Christ Jesus my Lord: for whom I suffered the loss of all things, and do count them but refuse, that I may gain Christ, and be found in him, not having a righteousness of mine own, even that which is of the law, but that which is through faith in Christ, the righteousness which is from God by faith.[15]

Their own great Fellowship is a resource to all Christian persons—the vast body of His followers throughout the centuries in all lands, the church universal and invisible, the fellowship of all believers, the mystical body of Christ, the Communion of Saints. Also, and not to be underestimated, a man finds within himself great unused resources, deeper levels of energy, capabilities, and potentialities, deeper insights and understandings, more beautiful memories and outreaching visions than he had realized. These lie just beneath the surface awaiting the releasing power of Jesus' great purpose. When that purpose becomes his own purpose a man needs to reach down into the inner reservoirs of his own resources, as did Pope Leo XIII, speaking as if to himself, "Rouse thyself, O Leo, endure the heaviest trials. Undertake the greatest burdens, for the everlasting God is with thee." The possibility of continuing effort and spiritual arousal are

[13] John 14:25, 26. Goodspeed translation.
[14] II Corinthians 12:9.
[15] Philippians 3:8, 9.

in the soul of man at every stage of his life experience. These even to extreme old age are resident there, as in "Prayer of Columbus" "A batter'd wreck'd old man, thrown on this savage shore, far, far from home," still had it in himself to cry,

> One effort more, my altar this bleak sand;
> That Thou O God my life has lighted,
> With ray of light, steady, ineffable, vouchsafed of Thee,
> Light rare, untellable, lighting the very light,
> Beyond all signs, descriptions, languages;
> For that, O God, be it my latest word, here on my knees,
> Old, poor, and paralyzed, I thank Thee.[16]

A YOUNG MINISTER'S PROBLEM AND PROGRAM

All young ministers have deep need of spiritual resources, for sometimes members of church boards put them to it for the faith that is in them, as in this illustration drawn from experience.

The chairman of the board of trustees speaks: "As members of the board of trustees, we would like to ask a few questions of our new pastor. We'd like to know what you feel we are driving at in this church of ours. We'd like to get our feet on the ground. Some of us got lost in those flights of yours about imagination in last Sunday's sermon. We are always glad to co-operate, of course, but all big ideas have to be brought to book, you know. Everything costs money these days, even religion. Every new plan has to be got into the budget and set down under one head or another. Every plan that's worth anything costs money and has to be financed. We like to balance the books each year with a tidy surplus. We always have. Just how are you planning to finance these new plans? What are the specific items in the larger program

[16] Walt Whitman. From *Leaves of Grass*. Copyright 1924, by Doubleday, Doran & Co.

for which money is needed, and how much money do you want of us for each item? And also, now that we're getting down to brass tacks, there's a point of view some of us board members hold that I'd like to state. I might say in passing that the make-up of this board includes as substantial a group of business men as there is in town—mature men of experience, sound judgment, and established positions. I suppose that is why we have been elected year after year. Run your eye down the list and see the banks and business houses we represent. A number of us are, as you know, from the older families of the community, which have been heavy contributors for years. We have taken close care of this beautiful property, seen to repairs and improvements, put in the new furnace and these beautiful new stained-glass memorial windows. We are proud of this church, proud of this town, proud of its local enterprises even if it can't claim to be a big town. We enjoy this church of ours. We like to come here to worship God and to eat our Wednesday night suppers.

"We have always met our own kind of people in our church, but lately we've been a bit bothered by the raft of new people you've been bringing in. Perhaps we shouldn't be critical, but you don't seem to realize they are not really our type. They are, most of them, here temporarily on these government projects or are small business people. Many of them are really only laborers, migrant laborers, and there's a lot of riffraff among them. We can't give them credit at our banks or stores. And then, besides, all this mob of their children! They've been scratching up the furniture and tromping on the lawn. They simply must be kept under better control. These people won't stay here long, they'll not contribute to the church, and they'll never have any social standing. They're no better than the poor folks over beyond the tracks. They ought to have a little chapel of their own. The government ought to provide it for them. We don't like to say so, but the fact is, some of our wives don't want to receive these people socially. Yet it doesn't seem right for us not to, if you're going to take them into our church.

"Of course we do appreciate your being such a hustler. You'd have even made a good businessman, and we do want to co-operate with you to the best of our ability. I didn't intend to make so much of a speech, but I guess it's better to get it all off my chest since we're getting down to brass tacks here tonight. How about it, boys? Am I right?"

"Okay, Jim! One hundred per cent right old boy!"

Meditative phase. Young minister sits long silent, ruminating as follows: "Well, this is one of the happy moments of life! Spring zephyrs, where have you gone? Divine afflatus, where art thou? Can't seem to imagine anything right now. But cheer up! This also will pass. This must be one brand of the trustee-mind speaking, the secure American skeptic mind, ultra-cautious on religious plans, but never so hard-fisted as it sounds when bearing down on a young minister's new ideas. What this sort of mind really wants is to preserve the status quo, to dominate this situation as it does others, to be teased to be benevolent as it is by the children at home and by the junior partners at the office. Not all these trustees have it, of course, but the rest of them close up when Jim gets to going. Bill here is all right, except when Jim has him under his thumb. Jim must have something on him to cow him down like that.

"Strange quirk this, to distort a fiduciary relationship into a means of financial domination and personal power. It's the same quirk that distorts so many relationships of trust in American life, outside of the churches as well as in, when money control gives power to men. Some of them are just not big enough men to stand it. That must have been at the bottom of those Louisiana scandals, starting, probably, with about the same attitudes some of these trustees have. Still,

115

our trustees are the finest of men personally, except for the hard-driving practices they have caught in the businesses in which they made their money. They are right of course about the budget. I must be more careful about that. Perhaps I ought not to get so stirred up about welcoming all these wonderful young people who have moved to town with their children, what the church could do for them and what they could for the church. But heavens and earth! Money isn't all there is to a Christian church. These fellows just think about money, money, money. But money and property aren't the big things in Christianity—not by a long shot. The love of it leads to something quite different. And so Jim puts the program and the budget all up to me, as if I were either a big boss like he is, or a visiting salesman who hadn't sold himself to them. But I mustn't get bitter about it, for I know that at heart they are good men. Well, I've been silent here a long time, so now I must reply. God help me!"

Action phase: "Gentlemen, you may well believe I welcome your interest in our church so frankly expressed. I appreciate it greatly. It is wonderful to find such a group of men who want to get down to brass tacks with the program and the finances. I recognize at once the need of our making that program specific and seeing if and how we can get our new hopes into the budget, and, by your leave, get them out again alive. With your help perhaps we can! I'm sure we all want to do our part. I do appreciate your pledge of co-operation. I pledge you mine. You may be sure we will all have to count on each other to fulfill these pledges when we have a few little matters cleared up between us.

"I don't like to raise what might seem to be a technical point to begin with, especially with such an able lawyer present; but I do suggest we remember the differing functions of this board and of the session which, as I understand it, controls the spiritual matters of the church, the program

116

of our activities. The function of this board, if I understand it correctly, is the care of church property and the raising of the funds necessary for the program upon which the session, rather than this board, decides. Personally, I am not too keen about dividing the spiritual from the temporal in church matters. The function of this board, however, is perhaps the first brass tack we need to drive in together. I'm sure all our membership appreciate the efficiency with which your proper functions have been exercised, the beautiful condition of the properties, and the expertness with which our finances have been handled.

"The specific points in the program, with your kind indulgence, I plan to discuss with the session next week Tuesday, so that when these points come to you, they will constitute the program of the representatives of the church as a whole, duly chosen for that purpose. The session has been making careful studies of the possible services our church can render to the people of this whole city as it now is, and in co-operation with other churches. They will doubtless prepare the budget on the basis of all the needs as they see them; and after it has been fully discussed by them, it will come to you in due course. I feel sure there will be plenty of volunteers to help us raise it if the program is courageous enough and worked out democratically enough. I shall have more to say about the relation of money to religion when we are ready to present the budget to our whole membership.

"But may I say a word, Mr. Chairman, about certain points you have raised? I'll be brief, for I know you all have other engagements this evening, and I must not trespass on your time. I think we do, perhaps, have differing ideas about the kind of group this church is and ought to be. Of course we all rejoice in the beauty of these fine properties, but I suppose we must remember they are not here primarily for landscaping purposes or civic ornamentation. They are here as a means to an end. It is Christ's church rather than our church and His program we seek rather than merely one of our own making. As for the new people who are now coming in—I can't find that He ever made much reference to any old established first families in Jerusalem, and some He did make were, as I remember it, not altogether complimentary. They, of course, had not been exposed to His ideas very long.

"He seems to have been more interested in a rather ungainly lot of folks more or less disheveled by life, poor folks and jailbirds of one sort or another, and blind people whom He was trying to get out of their prison houses, folks who had been tumbled about a good deal. They must have been like some of our businessmen who went under during the depression, our unemployed, and all the different kinds of migrants we now have in such numbers in America—dust-bowl emigrants and others, people who have to pull their children out of school and church every few months if indeed they ever get them in at all. They must have been like our own poor folks over beyond the tracks who don't have any kind of credit anywhere. I may have it all wrong, gentlemen, but these mere laborers and these little businessmen and their families, and those you call riffraff seem like the people He cared most about and really wanted in His company. And as for the children, I don't see how they can have a good time in any church or any home without scratching up some of the furniture, at least in the children's rooms. Half a dollar's worth of paint will fix that up all right. I'll put it on myself. If it's children or furniture, gentlemen, you'll have to count my vote for the children. They are the important persons here, as I see it, they and their mothers and the young fellows and their brides or sweethearts who are trying to hang on to their Christian ideals in the midst of the business world as it is. They are the sort He was concerned about. Just ordinary people counted most with Him—all sorts of ordinary people.

I've lately been rereading my New Testament and studying that point. Why don't you try it, Mr. Chairman? It wouldn't hurt you a bit!

"I really don't see how we can trim His big ideas down so that they just fit our size in a small American town like this. The more work we do on His ideas the more changes they are going to make necessary in our ideas. I suppose He must have been a pretty dangerous Person with those new ideas of His about everybody's life being sacred, one man as good as another in the sight of God, about the whole human family's need to stick together and keep the peace instead of getting mad and flying off the handle. His disciples need to battle all the time against disease and every kind of wrongness, just as He did right up to the high spots in Jerusalem. It's no mere local program, gentlemen. It's for Asia and Africa and Europe as well as for every small town in America.

"Sometimes when I get all fed up with organization details, I seem to hear Him say, 'I didn't live and die for such things either. Can't the people in my church see that there's a great enterprise afoot in the world in my name? These ideas of mine are the most revolutionary ideas men ever got hold of. I came that all people everywhere might have Life and have it abundantly.'

"I keep saying to myself, 'Haven't the churches and their ministers got to learn to take people as the doctors do—poor or rich, dirty or clean, immoral or moral?' Most doctors seem really to believe all human beings are important just because they're human. The churches have got to come to that, too, as I see it.

"And now, since we're being frank with one another, let me say I shall do everything I can to correct the personal faults of which I am painfully aware. I know I make mistakes, and I need your help. I welcome your frankness, and I know you want me to be equally frank with you. I'm sure

you couldn't have been intending to suggest that I cut down
the great ideas of Jesus so as to make them easy and comfortable for us to live with. The one thing we must not do is
to take His thought and dwindle it. That I could not know-
ingly do and will not do. As I study my New Testament, I
say to myself, 'His program has to be our program!' As long
as the people of this church let me stay here and share my
life with you, my program will be just as close as I can make
it to His program. When you get home, please read Luke
4:18, 19, and you'll get it straight."

Meditative pause again. Bill whispers to Jim: "That's
great stuff, Jim. We haven't had a minister who knew his
stuff like that in years. He's got something we all need
most awfully. He's got the straight of it, Jim. We've been
wrong at a lot of points. The truth is, we're prettty much
all wrong! Let's own up and tell him so and back his
program."

Jim whispers to Bill: "Maybe so, Bill, but it will take a
terrible turnover in this town to do it. You know what's
under the surface here as well as I do. You know where you
and I really are, and the side deal we've been pulling. Don't
get swept off your feet, Bill. We need time to fix our affairs
up a bit before we say anything. We've got to protect our
reputations and positions, whatever we do. But possibly we
might go around together tomorrow night and see the Dominie alone. So long, Bill. See you tomorrow."

"Well, goodnight, Dominie, Good night, gentlemen. I
must be going. I'm already late for another engagement."

Our program," as stated the following week by the young
minister at the open church meeting: "Dear Friends, in
considering the courageous program which we have now
adopted unanimously for the year ahead—the program we
have all worked through so carefully together, thanks to
the session—we are well aware that the budget it calls for is

three hundred dollars more than that of last year. That's a sizeable sum for a church which includes so many young married people who have to figure closely to make ends meet. But if I understand the spirit of our church this year, there is a new enthusiasm to make our fellowship the most outreaching and friendly it has ever been. We must include all the new-comers in the government projects and all the transient young people. We must make everyone feel the reality of our interest in him.

"With our new features we now have quite a program. It includes our 'Mr. and Mrs. Club' of young couples which has grown so fast we can hardly keep up with the new members; our men's brotherhood with its frankness and honesty in discussion of the social problems which affect the welfare of our people; our support of the county health program; our unemployment relief and our informal employment service; our work for undernourished children; the new games we have all learned to play together with our boys and girls; the women's services to mothers in special need, with medicines, layettes, and hours of personal attention. These and the other new features in addition to our regular services seem to have won such approval that I have every confidence our canvass for support will put us over the top. Volunteer workers and pledges in advance are already coming in. The money is important, of course—we can't go forward without funds. But we all know that the spirit of fellowship and our own commitment to the program are even more important than the money. We know that downright honesty with ourselves and with one another, our faith in the Eternal, the rightness and the faith He expects in us and of us—these are the great resources of any group of followers of Christ. They mean power. Money isn't the big thing. The really important resources of any church are people who believe in the world-wide program of Jesus, believe in one another and in God.

I often think of Him as the great I Am, the spirit of Universal Love that supports us all and upholds us all, as if He were the great base of a living pyramid, with the fine togetherness of Christian fellowship making the body of that pyramid, and each of us an individual "I am" at the apex of that pyramid, the Eternal flaming up in all of us and in each of us. If every one of us keeps that flame alive in his heart we shall succeed. We need never fear for the future of our fellowship or for the final victory of the ideals of Jesus if we commit everything we are to Him in faith and outreaching love. Just as in our personal lives perplexities are being eased by the deep understanding we give to each other, so all the perplexities of America and the world can finally be solved by men and women who make use of spiritual forces. Courageous faith and action by people who care about other people will establish justice and love in communities like ours. The realm of love shall some day be established everywhere."

Late bulletin: "Budget already oversubscribed. Returns still coming in."

FOUR FUNCTIONS OF A
PERSON-MINDED MINISTER

VI

THE MINISTER AS PERSONAL COUNSELOR

REALIZATIONS ABOUT PERSONS AS INDIVIDUALS

PERSONS *need personal attention*. Persons are unique individuals. They need attention one by one. Obstetricians, trained nurses, and especially mothers understand this well. You can mechanize the mass production of motor cars by the thousands, attending only to points of junction in the process and to smooth running of the system as a whole. Individual cars receive little attention. They seem to get started best that way. They run themselves off the inclines all pepped up and ready to go. A litter of pigs presents important parallels in the animal world. But a young mother with her first baby soon discovers the uniqueness of a human being and the need for individual care. Even identical twins are found upon inspection to be strikingly different, and the world-famous quintuplets are five delightfully distinct personalities.

Mass handling rarely satisfies any individual. A normal person does not like to be a mere unit in a mechanical system. No young girl likes to be one of a thousand units of production, to work at machine number 867 for long hours under the watchful eye of commercialized regimentation, and then go back to a drab room in a long row of cheap little houses owned by "the company." Human beings, especially young feminine persons cannot stand depersonalized treatment and impersonal settings. They ought not to. It is against human nature. "Nobody really cares about me!" such a girl says to herself in her lonely room as she tries to satisfy her barest needs on her meager wages, if and when she is employed. She is silently saying to society, "What about me? When does anyone give me a coming-out party?" She is symbolic. She must have individual recognition. She has a right to it. She was born that way. She doesn't want attention just for the sake of it. Oh no! It's part of a woman's life history, a stage in the game. Stupid society! Can't it understand? The repercussions of the present mechanical system may not be visible on the smoothly rouged faces of the factory and sales girls who are caught in it. But they show up in the feverish pursuit of nothing to take the place of something never known. They reveal themselves sooner or later in nervous tensions, in emotional instability, in substitutes for marriage denied or long delayed, in substitutes for a home, for a husband and babies of one's very own.

Older persons who try to work out their personal destinies in the midst of the mechanical roar or the lonely chill of a depersonalized society also need help to negotiate the mammoth forces that shoot them hither and yon. Corporations with standardized national services often transfer their personnel abruptly. One young Cornell engineer and his wife, for example, have had to pull up stakes seven times in five years. Thousands have been dropped into the ranks of the unemployed with scant notice. Society has suddenly gone wholesale at the very time when local ties, subsistence farming, and independent homemaking have been cut down, and people's need for aid in individual adjustments greatly increased. Just now the quantity productionists and the regimentarians are having their day. Mass production and distribution mean profits for them. Money and power mean luxurious idleness for their pampered daughters. But the end of all that is not yet. Some of the daughters of the rich will not sleep on in idleness forever, and many discerning leaders in social agencies, in church and labor groups, are taking a hand in righting social wrongs. Everywhere individuals want to be validated as persons, want personal consideration and all the basic human satisfactions. This is as true for powerful men who run the steam shovels on great construction jobs as it is for children and for girls in factories and department stores. A basic realization about persons is that they want and must have consideration, one by one.

Persons are complex. It is natural for persons to want personal consideration from other persons. This want is easier to see than to satisfy, however, for the satisfaction of it involves a vast amount of wisdom and effort. This is due not alone to the enormous number of people who need attention nor to the fact that each is a special creation with special needs. It is also due to the fact that each person is a highly complex organism in himself. Heredity and environment have both played their parts in making him so. To understand people necessitates knowledge about them. To aid them adequately requires training and skill. The complexity of persons is more and more clearly recognized the more carefully they are studied. Jack at seventeen seems, at first blush, easy enough to understand. His superficial differences from Tom are easily discernable; but to think of him as "just another boy," one of many young people who are all "pretty much alike," easily understood and easily cared for, is a lazy-minded fallacy. There are elements of mystery in every person, in the young no less than in the old.

Any minister can get a fresh sense of the complexity of even the human body and its care by going into his physician's library and thumbing through his volumes on anatomy, physiology, surgery, and medicine. Hundreds of articles in medical journals every month disclose a running stream of fresh discoveries about that complex organism and how to keep it in health. So with all the sciences and arts related to persons—psychology, sociology, history, education, religion, and the like. They reveal the complexity of persons in themselves and in their life settings. Each person is discovered as a growing organism, highly developed out of a primitive past, complicated in structure, widely related to others, habituated in action yet singularly capable of change, able to make extraordinary adjustments and to fulfill specialized functions. Each in normal health is a springboard ready for adventure, a vehicle of knowledge, a potential flame of aspiration. The human mind, still so little known, is to be recognized as the most complex organism in the universe. Less than a century of scientific study has been brought to bear upon it. Earth, air, fire, and water, fish, flesh, and fowl, automobiles and airplanes are all simple compared to persons with their mysterious mentality. Every month adds some significant fact to our knowledge about them. It is essential, then, for humility's sake and for patience's sake to realize that our knowledge about them is still in rudimentary state, that intelligent aid to persons requires an art of ministry which is as yet in its infancy. This also is a basic realization.

Persons change and may grow. Another basic understanding is that people themselves are changing continually. There are, of course, dwarfs and morons who for different reasons do not grow beyond certain physical or mental stages. They stop growing at fixed points. But pretty much everybody else is endowed with a strange plasticity of body and mind, a pituitary something in the protoplasm which makes them, as we say, "grow up." In normal persons bodily growth is counterparted by mental and spiritual maturation. Not everybody grows up smoothly, developing through successive stages to maturity. Yet everyone changes with the flight of time, moves in some direction, and all normal persons have the capacity for growth. This is clearly revealed whenever they grow to be more and more highly developed persons. It does not yet appear what any boy or girl, what any man or woman may become. "We are free upward" once said John Dewey in a course in psychological ethics. Normal persons can mature, not alone in bodily growth, but also in emotional stability, in mental grasp and spiritual insight.

Look more carefully at the factor of change in the life situations of persons, for changes in situations interact with changes in persons. Everyone of these highly organized and highly mobile persons finds the fringes of his relationships with men and things changing every instant as he moves through the multiple reels of his own motion picture. This is not alone by reason of time flight. It happens also because of external forces, physical and social, which impinge upon him from without as well as by reason of combustible forces which erupt within. Visualize this man just hearing that the savings of a lifetime have been swept away. Watch this newly prosperous young husband and wife in their petty pleasures and selfish luxuries growing daily more estranged. "Why does this boy react so sharply against his home?" asks his autocratic father, who is too close to his own question to see himself as the chief reason for the boy's reaction. Or see this woman with the gleam of spiritual victory in her eyes after long facing of inevitable surgery for cancer, ready now for the unpredictable outcome. Persons are always persons in changing situations. As a matter of fact, they are persons in very many situations changing rapidly or slowly all the time they are alive. This also is a basic realization. Persons change and may mature in the midst of changing life experiences.

Inner changes are most meaningful. Again we recognize the drama of life in distinction from its melodramatic elements, the inner forces as more significant than the forces impinging from without. This does not mean that the external forces are unimportant. They may coerce a man into routine behavior. They may indeed maim him for life or snuff him out in a trice. More meaningful, however, to his spiritual growth are the inner attitudes, choices, decisions, and aspirations. These chiefly determine character. The inner person has dynamite in his hands. Indeed he is dynamite and when aroused may do great things. These things he may do though the body in which he lives be crippled; he may do even greater things because of his handicap. The potentiality for arousal within a man is one of the distinguishing marks of a person, the mechanistic behaviorists to the contrary notwithstanding. High spiritual arousal is often the mark of a significant person. To be able to apply the power of a quickened will, to overcome privations and handicaps, to reach out for the great resources—these all indicate a high potential for significant change. The dynamic of ideals, purposes and convictions operates here with strange combustible power. Normal persons can understand and organize themselves to high ends by their own inner choices if they will. The inner light still glows in those who tend it. This also is a basic realization on the part of those who discover spiritual dynamics.

> A spark disturbs our clod;
> Nearer we hold of God
> Who gives, than of his tribes that take I must believe.[1]

Perplexed persons need counsel. Relatively normal persons who live in average communities and country districts are those with whom a Christian minister primarily deals. He assumes that most of them are capable of coming to some degree of awareness about their own facts of life and of acting constructively in relation to them. This he expects they will do chiefly by use of forces available within themselves. These inner forces a minister would aid in quickening—these inner

[1] Robert Browning, "Rabbi Ben Ezra."

dynamics that release from bondage to power. Inescapably, therefore, he must come to grips with the first-hand problems of individuals in their life needs. Continuous facing of the issues imbedded in those needs will deepen his awareness as to where people actually are in the story of their lives. Some he will find prosperous and complacent, some cruelly acquisitive, some weak and vicious, others suffering but brave, having wrested inner peace and beauty out of their suffering. He will discover many who handle themselves effectively as new facts come hurtling at them, who utilize with forethought their resources, material, social, and spiritual.

Others—many others—are baffled in the modern world, unable to meet the issues life presents to them. A nurse in a hospital saw the outline of this chapter. She ran her eye down the list of headings, rested on the words, "Perplexed people need counsel," and said: "That is the big point. Almost everyone I know is perplexed, not just here in the hospital by sickness and by all the changes death brings when it comes. Everywhere I go I find people perplexed by life. Most of them do not know what to do about their problems." That statement represents the experience of many ministers of all types who come into realistic relationships in the common life. It does so for those who have shared in our searches.

These ministers have described the perplexities of some hundreds of persons confidentially, so noting them that identities have been scrupulously concealed while perplexities have been revealed. Two piles of papers a foot high on the author's desk record them. These give fresh glimpses into the veiled story of our common life. They reveal, of course, the ancient sources of human tragedy—storms, fires and floods, hunger, disease and accidents, ignorance, laziness and selfishness, evil doing in relationships, the loss of loved ones, and many other age-old sources. These records also reveal in the factor of social change additional sources of bafflement. These are as real, if not as dramatically tragic, as when a native people is forced to vacate its homeland at the sudden behest of an alien conqueror. Social changes on many fronts now coerce men to live in a country which they know not and to work with tools they do not understand.

Here in our records are the stories of men and women who crave security but are faced with stark unemployment and abject poverty. Others have unjust returns for their labor and no more security of tenure than day-wage cotton-pickers who are shuttled back and forth in great trucks between Memphis slums and Arkansas cotton fields if and when they are needed. Here also are stories of able-bodied boys who can make no work contacts of any kind, nor secure the education which is supposed to foster security, except perhaps through the C.C.C. Here are young men and women so insecure they dare not marry, or being married dare not have children. Here also are older people cut off at an age point as if it were a death date. All this is taking place while the banks have great surplus accumulations waiting to be loaned "on security." Such insecurities cut deeply into the very souls of persons, shake their faith in themselves, bring them to a sense of inferiority, to loss of mental and spiritual fortitude. They need wise counsel from counselors with resource-power.

Here are the records of young people eager for mutual response in love and marriage, for a home and parenthood. Cheap substitutes are adopted when these are denied. But not alone does the insecurity of a long economic depression baffle them. The very set-up of modern urban life thwarts and distorts their desires for intimate response. Crowded tenement rooms and tiny apartments drive their privacies out into public places and commercialized resorts. Those same desires are blocked in other ways by rural isolation. The rythmic responses prevalent in friendly old-time workrooms are not fostered under a piece-price factory system which drives for maxi-

132

mum production at minimum cost. And so with the simple games of groups into which team play and the love of adventure entered—these are made to seem dull beside the fictitious glitter of night club offerings. Social changes in many areas like these now spell bafflement to those who long for intimate response in conditions that foster wholesome happiness. They need responsive counselors who understand all this.

Here again are younger and older people alike who are eager to share in altruistic groups, to espouse causes that might bring justice to beleaguered peoples. They are baffled at the social power of traditions and prejudices, the sterility that exists in many social institutions—not least in some of the churches to which they went as children. They are perplexed by the old and new exploitations of women and children, of poor and ignorant people. They are amazed at the ruthlessness of cruel men in positions of power, at the trickeries of venal men in business and politics. They are saddened by racial and social scorn and the sequences of injustice that are unrelieved. They see no adequate reason for the multiple forms of governmental regimentation nor excessive taxation for public funds coercively collected and wastefully spent. Many of the bravest younger men rebel against the encroachments of the military machine. Their deep loyalty to the best in the national life is thwarted by the knowledge that if war should come again they would be coerced into slaughtering and being slaughtered or persecuted as conscientious objectors. Socially minded persons are thus revealed as among the most perplexed. They crave great wisdom from courageous counselors.

Here also are recorded the perplexities of many persons who long to know more deeply the meanings of life that outlast all frustration and even death itself, to find eternal truth in a living faith to be expressed in lives of peace and beauty. Many are beaten back by their own mistakes, by long-drawn illness, by loss of loved ones, and by the whole vast mass of human suffering which they share as in a fellowship profound. No sterile formulae of salvation satisfy them, nor outworn dogmas which are meaningless in their experience. In loneliness behind shuttered windows or in thronging crowds on city streets, in the burning heat of isolated labor on remote farms or in the roar of factory workrooms, they wrestle often in silence, for their faith in God and life. They need great-souled men and women of faith as counselors who know for themselves the way, the truth, and the life, and who can lead others reverently, one by one, to the Answerer of human need. Can person-minded ministers make answer?

REALIZATIONS ABOUT PERSONAL COUNSELING

Some ministers dedicate themselves to this great art. To the great art of personal counseling—the pastor's art—they are now dedicating themselves anew, humbly seeking to understand and practice it more thoroughly than ever before. They are no longer willing to deal ignorantly with human needs, to mouth over sterile platitudes, or to rush about on matters of secondary importance. They are committing themselves to a deeper study of these needs as they exist today and to realistic efforts to bring every available resource both human and divine to the meeting of the needs of individual persons.

Are all ministers dedicated like that? Frankly they are not, and many perplexed people have come to realize this. The minister whose first attention is on his system of organization or his Sunday morning eloquence, on the embellishment of his ritual or the richness of his architecture, on his own denominational advancement or any other means to ends does not have it in him to give much attention to people, one by one, especially if they are "unimportant" people. Yet real attention is the thing people want, understanding, personal

134

attention. Putting it bluntly, some very intelligent and very busy ministers have not yet got the point that persons are ends in themselves, that ordinary persons have a mysterious actual sanctity all the more real because they carry no visible marks of distinction. They, in their life situations, are infinitely worth attention.

The most priceless thing any minister has to give, the thing that is uniquely his own, is his mind-time. Nobody else can ever duplicate that, the intelligent self-giving that might make him truly creative in relationships, a vehicle of great resources. As a plain matter of fact, the last thing some ministers want to have confront them is a person in a problem situation, a misunderstanding in a family or an unemployed boy. Their minds do not focus there and grip the facts. They evade and camouflage and step aside for more urgent matters. But person-minded ministers begin their ministry right then and there, and they stay with the people to their end of days. They follow the career of a pastoral ministry with an exhilaration no fishing trip could excel. People—ordinary people—are exciting to them, like a new adventure to an explorer, like a new patient with an unknown malady to a diagnostician, like a new client with a tangled problem to be analyzed to a lawyer—only more so. They see each person coming to them for help as one of those whom Jesus counted sacred. They say to themselves, "This room of mine must now be like an altar above which fly invisible seraphim crying, 'Holy, holy, holy!'" It comes down to a matter of insight and realization; to a principle, which, once adopted, alters the weekly and monthly schedules and reorients one's whole life around persons. (K. T. reoriented his life like that to marvelous results.) Persons, one by one, are worth a minister's scrupulous attention.

A human destiny in one bit of counseling. Whenever a person in a real situation comes in the minister's door, or the minister goes in his door, the minister is on the spot, though he may not realize it. Such an occasion is no simple affair. He comes to his testing just as certainly as a surgeon does when he enters the operating room after the ambulance has clanged up to the hospital's emergency door. Like the surgeon he must be ready for anything and able to handle what he finds. It may prove to be only a case of slightly wounded egocentricity or one of imminent nervous breakdown, or it may be a session with a violent father whose unmarried daughter is soon to have a baby. He must be prepared for the unexpected. He must know the art of counseling and be prepared to practice it with sure and steady hand.

He must realize in advance something of what is involved whenever two persons face a life situation together. Gradually he comes to understand that when Jack, for example, comes in the door the whole of him comes in, though he may show only a little bit of himself at first and that bit behind some sort of mask and with a hazel twig in his hand by which he feels out the situation. He sees at once that Jack is a person different from all other persons and that he is, indeed, many persons. All the different psychological personalities which William James described in his famous passage about the "me's" are there inside his skin. All his ancestors are there, especially his parents. His babyhood, his boyhood, all his early experiences step in with him. His schoolmates and his teachers come in too. Whatever his brothers and sisters, his aunts and uncles, his early companions have done to him; whatever society and social change and social institutions have done to him; whatever he has done or has failed to do with himself —all are there. His abilities and interests, his fears and prejudices, his loyalties and hopes are also there. Along with these there might be a special fondness for Mary Elizabeth or Helen Sue. There is also within him at this moment some special tension pulling this way and that. He and Mary Elizabeth

136

want to be married, perhaps, but he can find no job. Some inner tension guides the divining rod as he moves it to and fro, feeling out the potential counselor.

Has the counselor eyes and ears to sense all this? Has he spiritual tentacles wherewith to begin to understand both the boy and his situation? It is part of the counselor's responsibility to be in readiness for such an experience with some sense of the human destiny involved. Life may be changed forever in this hour by a word, a gesture, a discerning silence, a penetration of understanding never before encountered by this boy. The greater the counselor the greater the potential meanings. Words may be spoken, quiet questioning words that go to the very spot of need, words that are freighted with wisdom, comfort, or releasing power. Listen to Marian Earle, the betrayed shop girl whom Romney Leigh rescued from the London slums.

> "She could say the words,"
> She told me, "exactly as he uttered them
> A year back, since in any doubt or dark
> They came out like the stars, and shone on her
> With just their comfort. Common words, perhaps
> The ministers in church might say the same;
> But *he,* he made the church with what he spoke:
> The difference was the miracle," said she.

The counselor may be sure of this: he will not escape the potential demands of such an hour with routine attitudes, nor with any kind of inattention or evasion. All that he has and is, his every resource of knowledge and experience, his every gift of insight, his every ounce of stamina, his whole philosophy of life and spiritual wisdom may be called upon in this unpredictable hour. It is always potentially a great occasion when two such persons meet: so like lightning may the flashes of insight come; so like the clearing of thunderclouds before the sun may fear or anger or perplexity disappear; so like the final discovery of light in the darkness of night, after long groping, may the answer disclose itself. The experienced counselor has learned by his own mistakes and blindness, as well as by the lights that have shone in previous problem hours, to sense a little of the potentiality of any moment when a counselor and another person meet in an honest search for answers to the issues of life.

What is a ministers purpose in counseling? Let us be clear as to what he seeks to achieve lest it be confused with other functions and lest he have imputed to him ideals which he cannot in good conscience hold. As we understand it, his purpose is to understand persons in their life situations ever more clearly and deeply, to aid them similarly to understand themselves, to help them organize themselves for their own fullest development and usefulness, and to utilize all their resources, especially the resources available to them through Jesus.

This is no new purpose. It has long characterized discerning pastors. Note where it locates responsibility—with the counselor, to understand and aid but not to assume direction, not to control or to dominate the other person. It locates responsibility on the other person, for that is where, sooner or later, life locates it and where it has to be left if he is to become capable of increasing self-direction. If the other person is an advanced neurotic or psychotic, needing confinement and custodial care, the degree of responsibility that can be located upon him is greatly reduced, of course; but such acceptance of responsibility as can be secured even there is sought and valued by those responsible for the care of such persons.

Dealing, as the minister does, chiefly with normal persons, he purposes to sustain and heighten the sense of responsibility in them and not to take it away from them by fostering de-

138

pendence upon himself. Habitually to cut down the sense of another's autonomous selfhood and subordinate him, or especially her, to subserviency is eventually devastating both to the counselor and the other person. The fundamental issue of personal autonomy, of capable self-direction, is at stake in the clearance of this point. Many a much petted or bossed boy or girl has learned of this necessity too late in life, to his sorrow. Many a tyrannical parent, autocratic college dean, factory foreman, or plantation owner, who might have been a counselor, has likewise learned it to his sorrow too late. Persons are always to be treated as responsible persons, not as pets or slaves. The priceless right to be treated as a responsible person may not be denied in a democratic society—least of all by ministers.

The other person must therefore not be allowed to throw off responsibility for his behavior upon others, upon the counselor, or, as he is prone to do with ministers, upon God. Counselors do well to be clear on this point early, before they add to the weight of forces already at work weakening character and emasculating personality.

Note also the implications of the spiral arc of growth. The recurrence of action-times and times for meditation is implied throughout our statement of purpose. The counselor expects no lightning flashes of character transformation, although he fully understands that a fundamental decision may be sharp and definite at a point in time and that great changes may follow rapidly upon a basic decision. But he knows that reflection and action must follow one another for permanent results.

As he seeks true method for himself, he will study with care the psychological and spiritual damages which have often been inflicted upon persons in the name of religion. He will find in use among many revivalists methods so essentially dishonest, so selfishly motivated, so palpably unfair and damaging to persons, that he can have no part nor lot with them. Since every person he deals with is a sacred person, so also is every complex of emotions, every man's mentality and high desires. He will maintain, even at cost of heavy criticism, his purpose to be honest with the spiritual integrity of others, refusing to coerce them emotionally any more than he would beat them physically.

Furthermore the counselor's ends are in the other person, not in himself. No starved hungers of his own are to be fed at the other person's expense. Few fully realize the prevalence or the dangers of such emotional parasitism. By means of it one's own egocentricity may grow to colossal proportions and other persons be made subservient to one's ends.

SUGGESTED STEPS IN COUNSELING PROCEDURE [2]

One characteristic of counseling method as here conceived, which sharply differentiates it from some other methods, is in its being, as fully as possible, a shared process. There are, of course, items of information confided to the counselor by friends of the other person, the nature and source of which cannot be shared with him as received. Neither does the counselor fail to maintain a considerable degree of reserve as to his own impressions as he proceeds. But aside from these two items the process may be quite completely a joint inquiry. This is more easily carried out with some persons than with others, especially when the degrees of complexity or strain are less acute. To share with another in a joint inquiry into

[2] This section is a summary of lectures on "The General Counselor and His Work" given by the author at the Hazen Conference on Student Counseling at Happy Valley, Lisle, New York, in 1934, edited by Professor Maynard L. Cassady of the University of Rochester, and privately printed in the conference report. Only main steps are touched upon in this summary. Chapters II-V in the present volume, however, aid in amplifying it. The principles set forth in those chapters and their application to wider areas of relationship grew out of the analysis of counseling procedure as summarized here.

a life situation aids the other person in taking an objective attitude toward himself.

Toward a point of view on counseling. The true counselor sees the other person always as another person, that is, as a subject, as Fritz Kunkel makes clear in his *God Helps Those.* Other persons are to be treated as subjects, not as objects, not as means to some end entertained by another. The attitude differentiates the approach of the counselor from that of the salesman, the newspaper reporter, the public official. This attitude prevents him as a counselor from indoctrination, from recruiting, from dominating, and from spiritual imperialism.

The counselor needs to reconcile within himself certain apparently opposite characteristics and attain in his personality a living synthesis: (a) of approachability and reserve, so as to be an open-hearted, wide-eared listener, but also a deep well, not a babbling brook; (b) of objectivity and at the same time subjectivity, in the sense of a full-flowing life of his own; (c) of disinteredness and concern. The counselor's focus of interest is in the other person; and his chief concern, therefore, is that help shall be given rather than that he be the one to give it. "Even more valuable than technical training and knowledge is the proper attitude—one must be interested in the sufferer." There must be also a synthesis: (d) of sensitivity and robustness; (e) of insight and accurate observation; (f) of patience and resourceful action; (g) of a knowledge of life as it is and a sense of the sacredness of personality.

Preliminary aspects of the counseling procedure. The general counselor, reviewing his experiences with several persons in problem situations, is aware of the uniqueness of each person and of the difficulty of rigidly classifying either situations or persons into standardized types. Each individual in his present situation is unique. Long case-histories and circumstantial material are seen as less important than the dynamics of the actual counseling process. Classifications always give less than the full truth. A few of the methods of classifying persons in situations are: (a) by the areas of experience in which difficulties arise; (b) by symptoms manifested in early interviews; (c) by types of causal factors; (d) by types of persons as extrovert or introvert; (e) by degrees of acuteness of the problem. Classification, however, is not a particularly urgent quest in counseling. To understand the individual person in his particular situation is the great essential.

Counseling experiences reveal certain major aspects of procedure. There is first the initial contact with the "other person" —or "O.P.," a term preferred to "counselee," "patient," or "client." Many informal contacts as well as those involved in teaching and administrative relationships are easily available to most of us. The impression made on the other person at the first interview is important. Such factors as an attractive, well furnished room, where a sense of friendly welcome is present, furnish a setting for the counselor. He should avoid hasty diagnosis, curiosity, emotional outbreaks, advice-giving, and his favorite panaceas. Observation by eye and ear, conjectures as to formative influences, and the establishment of rapport are essential.

It is important to have an understanding with the other person about records. The conversations may be wholly oral, or records may be kept privately by the counselor, or a record of findings may be made and kept jointly except for certain materials agreed upon from the first. A joint study of the developing records is made possible by the last method, and at the same time confidential materials are kept confidential.

Getting at the more objective facts. Basic in the counselor's procedure is securing the pertinent facts. He seeks these only for the bearing they may have upon the other person and his present or future life-situation. Guided conversation is productive.

THE MINISTER AS PERSONAL COUNSELOR

Good fact-finding is a shared process in counseling. The confidential biography lends itself admirably as a means for eliciting facts and discovering attitudes. This may include for a student an outline form, given him by the counselor, including name, age, home address, physical condition, inheritance, parents' occupation, home background, studies, grades, recreations, vocational experiences, hobbies, achievements, and the like. Back of any methods used for securing facts the insights and artistry of the counselor remain indispensable. There are other sources of information, such as school records, letters from friends of the other person, results of tests, rating scales, and special inquiries.

Getting at the more subjective facts. The more subjective facts may be conceived of on three levels: (a) those which are frankly spoken; (b) those secreted or suppressed; (c) those repressed. The general counselor does not attempt to deal with the last. These he leaves to the expert, to the psychotherapist. It is chiefly with the second, the secreted or suppressed facts, that the general counselor is most concerned. In approaching these inner areas of life there are great dangers of bungling and error. Only the right spirit, coupled with long and careful study and practice, brings competence. It is important that the other person be not made dependent upon the counselor but helped to gain and retain a sense of independence and ability to meet his own life situations.

The earlier autobiography, which gave the more objective facts, may well be followed when the time is ripe by confidential conversation about the particular persons who have been of greatest influence, such as parents or closest friends; experiences which have most shaped the inner life; fears, prejudices, interests, loyalties, ambitions, and other "inner facts." There is no standardized method. The interview varies with the counselor, the other person, and the nature of the situation.

143

In the field of the subjective factors, the general counselor recognizes that he lacks the expertness of the psychotherapist. Yet he must be able to recognize neurotic and psychotic symptoms and know at what point the expert psychologist, psychiatrist, or psychoanalyst should be called in. The general counselor will limit his counseling to relatively normal persons; his work is preventive as well as remedial. When crucial physical or mental problems arise, he needs to have access to experts to deal with the emergency.

Assembly and diagnosis of the data. The notes and records which have been jointly worked out by the two may now be studied together and other materials interpreted by the counselor. The more significant symptoms and causal factors, as mutually understood, can be reviewed and a confidential summary or epitome written down. Whether or no this be written out, the mutuality of the conclusions, to the degree to which mutuality is possible, is highly important. After the diagnosis is agreed upon, and after a period in which further observation, meditation, and insight play their part, there may be revision based on deeper insights and realizations until all pertinent facts are recognized as facts by both.

Acceptance and rectification—the immediate program. Realization of the truth which the joint diagnosis has determined must be followed by the acceptance of the facts as facts on the part of the other person. Certain unalterable factors in the situation, such as incurable physical deformities or the death of a loved one, must be accepted for what they are. Full acceptance of the unalterable is essential. But many factors in the situation as well as in the person are alterable. Habits and attitudes toward self or others on the part of the other person must be seen as part of the real self and as alterable. Certain habitual ways of responding in the past may be recognized as "bad," their effects realized, and new attitudes and habits begun. From the full acceptance of the diagnosis may arise a new determination, a will to change, an inner reassertion against the lethargic or inflexible tendencies which have crept in. Rectification of these elements, subject to change, may follow. The basis of such change lies in a new commitment. Hadfield says, "Freedom of the will can be assured only by commitment to the good or the ideal," or, as John Dewey says, "We are free upward."

There are two main phases of rectification: (a) that of attitudes, habits, and purposes within the person; and (b) that of actual personal relationships with others. Forgiveness may be sought and given, restitution made; faith and trust in others formerly feared or mistrusted may be established, and constructive co-operation set up with other persons in new relationships. The keynote is reconciliation with other persons looking toward a new and better society. Revenge, reprisal, hatred, fear, and egocentricity are to be sloughed off by faith, hope, and love.

The longer program. Persistent reeducation is needed, for long established habits and attitudes are not immediately transformed. Growth is gradual; and it requires, above all else, the transformation of purpose in released social living and the conscious choice of ideals and selection among conflicting ones. In the light of the new goals and with the aid of all the resources of religion, continued rectification of habits and attitudes proceeds.

A rethinking of the vocational choice and reworking of plans for achieving it grow out of the new purpose. But vocations are no longer as fixed in society as formerly. Many new vocations have emerged. The depression has created insecurity, and major vocational readjustments are now in process. Adaptability to changing situations, avoidance of overspecialization, readiness of mind to accept new opportunities are essential factors today in any true vocational adjustment.

145

Sustaining counseling relationships. Our discussion now returns to the procedure of the counselor. Once launched on the longer program, the other person is aided to move more and more on his own resources while the counselor "goes inactive." He should see the "O.P." less and less often, always however maintaining accessibility. This relationship may continue throughout a lifetime on the basis of genuine friendship. At times a specific review of progress and revision of plans for the future will be undertaken.

Concluding considerations. Counseling in its broader aspects is one method of establishing meaningful relationships between persons; it is a way of life rather than a separate vocation. It requires insight, training, persistent study, the devotion of time, the achievement of skill and spiritual maturity, but not necessarily any particular professional status.

Counseling experiences lead to a more realistic conception of and experience in the social situation. Confidential information about concrete personal problems deepens knowledge of social processes. Well-based social theories should grow out of such first-hand knowledge. Thus social reconstruction needs to be studied with reference to factors of personal experience. The clarification of the individual problems must be made in the light of social needs. Thus the new person emerges to aid in the reshaping of society. Ideally, he makes commitment to great causes to which his own actual experience in participating in that society has led him.

Religion is implicit in the entire process. The entire conference has moved in a deep spirit of religious devotion. There are no more releasing factors than the love of God in the lives of men and the concern of men and women for one another in attaining worthy personal quality and a just society. These religious resources are assumed throughout this series.

THE MINISTER AS PERSONAL COUNSELOR

THE MINISTER'S DISTINCTIVE FUNCTION IN COUNSELING

Is there a distinctive need for ordained ministers among the many agents of human therapy today? There are surgeons, physicians, and nurses for bodily ills. There are relief workers for material needs. There are social case-workers for family adjustments. There are Red Cross workers for disaster relief. There are counselors-at-law for tangled business affairs and the settlement of estates. There are consulting psychologists for the adjustment of mental mechanisms. There are teachers to guide the learning process. There are prophetic social workers and public officials to establish and maintain a favorable environment. All these persons, along with parents, neighbors, and friends, may be, and often are effective counselors.

Where does the ordained minister come in distinctively? He appreciates profoundly the services of all these other persons. Some of their special functions he himself may exercise, as need arises or if he have some special gift for one of them. But what is his own distinctive function as counselor?

The answer to this question arises out of the inner lives of persons, out of their basic desires, and peculiarly from the frustration of those desires. Therein lies their immemorial heartache—in the craving to know and achieve the fullest meanings of life. Therein lies their aspiration for beauty, truth, and rightness, for victory over all life's vicissitudes, for "the peace of God which passeth all understanding." For answer to these deep hungers, millions of persons still turn to ordained ministers. This is the minister's distinctive function with persons, one by one, to foster the inner light, the light of courage, aspiration, faith, and love. He is ordained above all else to transmit to them and foster in them the light that shone and still shines in Jesus. We turn for meditation, therefore, upon inner light and its quickeners—to Jesus and his kindling power.

A PERSON-MINDED MINISTRY

Despite the dark of human life there are all about men quickeners of light, as when in a summer evening one watches the rhythmic glow of tiny winged creatures incandescent from within. No scientist knows the source of that cool light, but it glows from within and casts illumination round about. It would be well to spend many a summer twilight hour silent in meditation in the midst of them. It would be well also if perplexed persons might spend hours of quiet with the Friends, thinking over this matter of inner light, and share in receiving the flashing communications they have in their times of silence.

But who are the quickeners of inner light? In the world of nature the sun is, of course, the mighty one.

> Who girt dissolved lightnings in the grape?
> Summered the opal with an irised flush?
> Is it not thou that dost the tulip drape,
> And huest the daffodilly,
> Yet who hast snowed the lily? [3]

Then there is sunlight that has been caught into persons. In rare persons there is a mysterious radiance, as in a certain gracious older woman long shut in by bodily infirmity, never able any more to leave her room. She has matched the radiance of the sun with a radiance of her own, a luminous quality which is there in that room authentically, whether the sun be shining in the heavens or no. A kind of healing therapy goes out to everyone who comes in to sit with her by her wide windows. Witty, vivacious, a lover of boys and girls, a lover of great books, she has made terms with pain and come off victor. In her is light. Well might her minister aspire to be

[3] Francis Thompson, "Ode to the Setting Sun." By permission of Dodd, Mead & Co.

such a light-bearer! Henry Drummond was like that as he lay suffering but saying to the friends whom the doctors let visit his bedside, "Don't touch me. I can't shake hands, but I've saved up a first-rate story for you." Rare Scotch stories they were, quickeners of radiance. In them and in such men as he, doubt it not, is light. All the humorous loveliness of life wherever it shines through persons has power of quickening. Humor lives in the same close quarters with suffering and sublimity. It has to, not alone for reasons of emotional relief and dramatic contrast, but because it may lead in the twinkling of an eye into some holy place.

Into the winsomeness of Jesus the suffusing power of humor must have entered. He who loved the children piping to one another and dancing in the streets, who jested about a great camel trying to scrunch through a needle's eye, must have had an inner radiance which brought new insights to persons in their need. The evidence all goes to show that He had a mysterious gift of healing power, supremely so. From person to person He went, understanding, quickening, healing them as if He held a magic light in his fingers—as indeed He did, because there was within Him an outreaching love for persons, one by one. That love has marked His true ministers always, priests and pastors through all the ages since He went about in Galilee. There is a heritage in the pastoral ministry in the cure of souls which is more and other than the cure of bodily ills, more and other than the adjustment of mental mechanisms, for it never underestimates the quickening of the inner lights as He quickened them. Scorn it as merely mystical if you will, but the results are dynamic in persons, ethically transforming, spiritually creative. Flame lights flame at His touch in the hearts of men today as through the ages. It is not by chance that we celebrate His birthday as a feast of lights.

A PERSON-MINDED MINISTRY

The more one senses the potentialities in great persons—a Michelangelo, a Savonarola, a Bach, a Shakespeare, the Brownings—the more does one reverence in the name of human destiny the possibilities in all other men and women, their aspirations and their insights. The person-minded minister knows that in dealing with human capacities the place whereon he stands is holy ground. Whatever gift of inner light or knowledge of life or quickening power he may have that draws men to him, these gifts he dare not call his own. Humbly sharing them as he would pass the bread and wine at sacrament, he understands that gifts like these are only to be shared, not kept. They are there as if by the presence of a mysterious visitor within his house, one who steals in silently with a brazier of live coals in his hands, puts it down, and then with only a gesture goes his way.

This is in some sense the reason why ministers want to be ordained, that the whole of life may be sacred to them—every life, their own and others. They desire to be consecrated by a laying on of the hands of men whose rightness and devotion to Christ they know and trust. Through an ancient lineage of ritual and love they sense Eternal Love coming to them like a flame direct on the wings of the spirit. They believe, under God, in the spiritual impartation of love direct from Jesus, sharable in a living fellowship with all who seek to achieve His purposes and transmissible to perplexed persons. Hence they believe in themselves as set in a holy calling, guardians of a sacred flame, transmitters of light. They want to live, not as having attained, but as pressing on "toward the mark for the prize of the high calling of God in Christ Jesus." They live in faith that the light of love will continue to abide within them and that they will be able to quicken in others living light. The proof will be found in the event, not otherwise. Shall there be a perpetual light, shining more and more unto the perfect day? The possibility of this —even a little through them—is in them a thrilling hope. They say to themselves,

> Ere it vanishes
> Over the margin
> After it, follow it!
> Follow the gleam.[4]

Finally, they live possessed by aspiration to be indeed creative in their relationships with others, true ministers of His grace. Humbly they say, "For their sakes I sanctify myself." Secretly they hope that at some evening hour when they come home wearied with ministering, the one who knows and loves them best may think of them as Agnes thought of Brand, her husband.

> Not mine alone: but whosoe'er
> In our great Household has a share,
> Each sorrowing son, each needy brother,
> Each weeping child, each mourning mother
> Of quickening nurture have their part
> At the rich banquet of thy heart.[5]

[4] Alfred Tennyson, "Merlin and the Gleam."
[5] Henrik Ibsen, Brand.

VII

THE MINISTER AS QUICKENER AND GUIDE OF VOLUNTARY GROUPS

MAN IS BY NATURE GROUP-MINDED

AS one goes deep into the lives of individual persons, one becomes more and more conscious of the network of social relationships in which they are enmeshed. No man liveth to himself or by himself. His social nature does not permit this; neither does organized society. In the first place he belongs to a family, and that is of course the most profoundly influential social grouping. Most boys and girls are so deeply imbedded in their family life that they find in it security beyond their understanding till long after independent maturity has come. Happily so. But they are more deeply marked by early family settings and influences than most of them ever realize. The family is one group from which it is impossible to resign. A boy's parents, brothers, and sisters, living or dead, continue to speak by radio voices he cannot switch off; for they are nearer to his inmost self than breathing, closer than hands or feet. He may run away from his home and change his name, but some day when he least expects a call from his father or his grandfather they bob right up inside of him. His mother or his sister puts a cool hand on his hot forehead when he thinks he is all alone in the silence of his far-away room or alone in his bunk aboard ship at sea. All the potent friends of his boyhood are there with him too. We are inevitably members of basic social groups from which we cannot resign.

To be group-minded is more than to be gregarious; and it

is more than to belong to some segment of humanity, male or female, young or old, rich man, poor man, beggerman, or thief. To be group-minded is to have the capacity for getting together with a few other persons in conscious face-to-face relations, or to have, with a few other persons who are more or less separated from one another, some common interest or purpose which may take precedence over face-to-faceness. Native group-mindedness binds people inevitably into little units of association. There may be two, ten, twenty, two hundred, or whatever the outer limit is at which a group ceases to play, confer, work, correspond, or think together. Groups are different from crowds, which are mere massy agglomerations of people. The persons in a crowd are chiefly unified, if unified at all, by common feelings. When these are intensified, they act in common, often with violence, but do not really confer, work, think, or even play together, as groups do. The human capacity of persons to do these things together is crucially important for person-minded ministers. Upon their understanding of groups, of audiences, of crowds, as well as of individuals, much of their success or failure in dealing with persons may depend.

GROUPS, MANY AND VARIED, ARE IN ALL COMMUNITIES

All sorts and kinds of groups have emerged in ordinary American communities—five men swapping stories around the coal stove in a village store, four ladies gossiping at cards, half a dozen boys playing "one old cat." These are informal, unorganized, ephemeral groups. Or there are organized groups more enduring in personnel and more highly unified by some common interest, like the finance committee of the local book club, weightily wrestling with the budget; the local Democrats in caucus assembled; the members of Lodge 23, F. & A.M., at least a few of them, going through the ritual; the little coterie of the local boss conferring in the smoky back room at "Jim's Place" getting ready to lead the people around by the nose some more; or the civic forum group where the intelligentsia say right out what they think, or what they think they think, or what they think they ought to think. Groups of every sort fairly infest American communities—sociable, political, industrial, cultural, religious. Their name is legion; their significance is profound. The English like to joke about this propensity of ours, as in their little jibe, "If three Americans fell out of an airplane together they would organize on the way down and elect a president, a secretary, and a treasurer before they got to earth."

GROUPS ARE INFLUENTIAL FOR BOTH GOOD AND EVIL

Groups show up the characteristics of people. They are intrinsically important in the unfolding of the human story. They uncover the basic drives that actuate their members. They exhibit characteristic patterns of social behavior. Few persons can be fully understood in the sterilized atmosphere of a prearranged personal interview. As a movie is more revealing than a still picture, a talkie than a silent one, so the give and take of group activities may reveal far more than systematic probing in a private interview. The latter may indeed, except in the hands of a skilled counselor, drive the inmost person quite out of sight. But group experiences show people up for what they are. Observation of them in unself-conscious group processes may add profoundly to that which the psychological analysis of individuals reveals. In their private personal relations Mrs. Axminster Aynesworth and Mrs. Tom Bigby may be as smooth as honeydew; but if both want to be elected president of the D. A. R., watch their electioneering attitudes and the methods employed by the other ladies on their behalf. Men are the same only different. Young people are like older people. Group games and conferences, shared work and joint thinking show them all up for what they are behind their elsewhere masked exteriors.

Bad and good alike come to the surface. In any lively game, indoors or out, in any free assembly where there is real discussion on real issues, or in the group execution of any demanding project, there may come into view aggression, dominance, avoidance, subservience, ambition, jealousy, bitterness, or hostility. At any moment in the sequence of events freedom to speak out, to act, to think with others may unlock inhibitions. Some petty irritation may release long pent hostilities. Quick retorts in anger or sudden blows may follow. Likewise the good shows itself: patience with slower moving minds, a well-bred temper, calm speech in low tones, a steady hand, the silent refusal to be barbed by innuendo, freedom from self-seeking, a gracious word of appreciation, a touch of humor, the ability to judge probable outcomes of group decisions, courageous commitment to common ends. People who have such marks of spiritual maturity are also revealed to those who have eyes to see objectively what happens in any creative group experience.

Many types of persons are also apt to be revealed: the evaders of issues and the slackers, the fearful and the avoiders of responsibility, the blow-offs and the blow-ups, the bluffers, the loud and frequent talkers, the quick-on-the-trigger optimists, the chronic pessimists, the supercautious, the slow reactors and those afraid to speak at all, the hypersensitive, the easily angered, the easily offended, the worriers, the grandstanders, the imitators and the sycophants—they may all be there in any sizable group. Along with them may also be well-poised persons of insight who see the underlying issues at stake in any discussion, the objective-minded and those who can weigh both sides of a question fairly, also clear-headed lifters who know how to await occasion or to act quickly, also those who know the characteristic attitudes and pet ideas of others and are able to estimate probable outcomes with high reliability. Though not unmindful of their own limitations, such persons know how to use all the group skills they possess.

Groups influence individuals profoundly. People find other people interested in the same things which interest them. They naturally join up with these around such interests. Groups thus widen acquaintance and explore common interests. They may affect habits of thought and speech, manners, dress, and morals. They may indeed become heighteners and deepeners of experience if the interests are wholesome ones. The reverse is also true. Even boys and girls are subject to dangerous cut-ins on character from unwholesome groups. When Jim takes up with a crap-shooting gang or joins a high school smut club whose members talk sex and begin to experiment promiscuously, something damaging happens to Jim. But if groups are wholesome in interest and membership, they cement fine friendships, heighten educational processes, and foster spiritual growth.

Groups influence society. They do so inevitably. Human social organization is immature. A clue to this is seen in the crudity of political control, which is still largely in the hands of a few individuals even for vast populations—little cliques who control communities, states, and nations. They do so arbitrarily in all totalitarian states. Any thoroughly widespread democracy of leadership is yet to be achieved anywhere. Everywhere the little power groups of men and women who gather around their leaders, consciously or unconsciously affect the state of society for good or evil. A little group of Tammany politicians, skillfully organized and enriched by graft, has kept New York City subservient over long periods of its history. Little groups of politicians in any Southern state can form a combination powerful enough to keep conditions industrially and culturally as they want them, at least for a time. They have done so over and over again. The same is true of most American cities and states, not forgetting California and Nevada. Such groups are unhorsed, if at all, by the leaders and members of other groups who have the courage to expose and convict "the gang."

Throughout society such groups powerfully affect our common life. Economic pressure groups—industrial, agricultural, regional, and racial—lie back of political parties and political combines. Chambers of commerce, employers associations, the farm bloc, labor unions, and innumerable others wield the group power of the special interest they represent. Other socially minded groups also powerfully affect our common life. They are organized to influence public opinion and legislative action independent of any special interest, and often in opposition to such interests. Political and economic measures in a democracy such as ours usually result from intergroup battles in which issues are drawn, possibilities explored, competing forces marshaled, compromises effected, and decisions arrived at by majority vote. The educational values of the democratic process in groups are perhaps the most important of all, for they advance the social awareness and the thinking powers of the people themselves. They change society by changing persons.

Groups may yield spiritual values that endure. Other groups in other areas are not less potent. They are perhaps more deeply so, as in education, literature, art, religion—all the permeative processes by which men and women not only express their own creative powers but also disseminate knowledge, train youth, refine taste, and enrich spiritual values among the people. By such conscious creative efforts great groups of workers share powerfully in shaping society. Still more directly aimed at the righting of evils, "social action" groups of varying types have come into being. By organized opposition to entrenched evils they are attempting to advance the arrival of a better state of society.

A PERSON-MINDED MINISTRY

Since creative relationships are central in our interest, we are intrigued by the power of constructive groups to yield cultural and spiritual results in persons, results that endure. The processes of fact-facing and solution-finding in socially minded groups may be indeed the most important of all social processes for achieving the realm of intelligent love. As thinkers and workers learn to think and work together they catch the spirit of team play. They prefer group results and group credit to individual rewards. They rejoice to share in increasing the durable social satisfactions in families and communities, in national and international affairs. They learn to aspire with others and to achieve with others. They learn in groups to practice with success, to make sacrifice hits, and to achieve results with socialized satisfactions. Realistic public worship, frank discussional hours in facing the actual issues of life, and group projects faithfully pursued are among the most essential processes for producing the character qualities in persons which Jesus seems especially to have desired. Such qualities in persons may become indeed the distillates of Christian social experience which shall eventually replace force with love in human affairs. To live and share in that faith is clearly in the mood of Jesus.

THE MINISTER MUST KNOW GROUPS

Any minister whose mind moves about in the deeper life experiences of his people, whose thought keeps focused there, will come to realize that groups are profoundly influential in shaping those experiences and in affecting social standards. He will want to know more about these groups, and wish for a deeper knowledge of the principles and laws which affect all groups, their structure, stability, and influence. He will not have had much help on this in his ministerial training, for there the emphasis in so-called "practical theology" has been primarily upon preaching. His functional training has been directed chiefly toward eliciting responses from audiences rather than guiding group processes of thought and action. There is indeed a tragic gap in the knowledge and training of most ministers at this point. Furthermore, they find themselves operating in church auditoriums, those rigid embodiments of audience psychology, built for listening crowds, with pews fastened to the floor to keep the people put—structures which make little provision for attractive conference rooms arranged for groups.

Nothing short of a revolution in ministerial training and in church architecture will give groups their true importance in the functional reorganization of American Protestantism. Suffice it, at this point, to say that no person-minded minister can ignore or postpone his study and use of group processes or of the principles which govern their successful operation. We grow more and more aware throughout these meditations that ministers must thoroughly know persons in their actual present-day life, just as a doctor must know anatomy and physiology and the diseases that afflict the people as well as the materia medica with which to heal them. Therefore the minister must know the actual and often bewildering group relationships of his people, and also the power of creative groups to transform communities and society.

In light of all we have been thinking about togetherness it is evident that a minister must bring to his study of all groups a friendly spirit and a constructive attitude instead of antecedent suspicion and hostility toward those which he considers might be inimical to the welfare of his church and people. Unless he approaches the whole matter constructively his knowledge will be tainted with prejudice. Most of us need to use at least one lobe of the brain as social psychologists, to study persons in groups objectively. If a minister does so with independence of judgment and at the same time with genuine interest, he will make friends, win respect, and widen his outreach. Why shouldn't he know how to circulate around town a bit, swap a yarn here and there, find out who is who and why, go to visit groups if invited, and go not always to make a speech. Why not become an unofficial ex-officio member of some groups without vote. If and as he does so he will discover great new values and dangers in groups. His heightened knowledge will help to socialize him and to enrich his ministry. A bit of careful memory work might also help him to understand groups more deeply.

The groups that have influenced him and his wife. In the mood of our meditation upon pastoral counseling, suppose a minister were first to rethink and realize the meaning of the group influences that have operated in his own experience and get his wife to do the same for hers. What have they been? What have they meant? What do they now mean for a man, for a woman? What are they in such groups as these: his own family, other families, clusters of childhood friends, a "gang" or "bunch" of boys at school, an athletic team, some small group interested in photography or in movies, in radio, airplanes, or motoring, in magazines or books? Did some church-school class, college fraternity or sorority, or group of young married couples leave a deep impression? Several important results may come from such a brief memory exercise. First, perhaps, he remembers the other persons who were in such groups. Though many are now far away, careful recall may yield the names of a half dozen with whom old friendships could be revived and a sense of fresh security in friendship deepened. There are never any friends like the old friends, especially some of them, and friendships deserve to be kept in repair. He also discovers some of the influences which those groups had upon him in his own developing life, fostering interests that have perhaps dominated all of his later experience or interests that proved to be of passing moment, like trial balloons quickly drifting out of sight. He discovers also some of the perennial interests that generally recur at the different age levels. Some of these abide through life; others, like playing "one old cat," fade away when certain stages of growth are past. He also becomes more keenly aware of group sources of good and evil, and of the mysterious contagions of influence that run through groups. He realizes freshly then the importance of ethical quality in one's associates, especially in the impressionable years. He begins to see more clearly also the prime importance of his own attitudes and activities as a potential quickener and guide of groups. But this hour of meditation will tend also to open his eyes more widely upon other group associations.

The groups in his church and the parish life. To recount the groups actually in or actively fostered by the church is a ten-minute matter at the most. They are seen as few among the many if account is taken of the friendship clusters, the clubs and societies, the unions and associations which are represented in the families of the parish. Any minister to be well informed about his people wants to know the array of these groupings much as a sociological survey would reveal them.

The groups in his community and region. A study of all known groups in his community or neighborhood brings a further extension of his knowledge to include other groups in other areas of the city or region, and of other schools of thought. For full social effectiveness in dealing with local politics, economic and religious issues, he must know the groups which are potential sharers in any future campaign for civic decency and social justice. The battles for rightness in which he will be engaged also necessitate his knowing the public enemy groups. Who are the gangsters and their leaders? Where do they make their headquarters? Where are the centers of vice and crime? Who are the well-dressed, smooth-voiced men and women who control them? What are their outlets and connections in the business world, their relations with merchants, police officers, doctors, nurses, lawyers, and bankers? These might be, perchance, members of his own church. They are usually silent as to their "professional connections," but they are able and possibly willing, if the minister is a thoroughly trustable person, to intimate to him the subsurface groups and leaders he needs to know about. He may indeed wake up to find that sons and daughters of his parishoners are being sucked into such groups or are in them already. He may then wish he had been better informed about these danger spots in his own community and region.

National and international groups. The circles widen to include political parties, labor unions, national and international associations, world movements, scientific and educational societies; their name is legion. Among them are the world church enterprises embodied in missionary and other societies, national and international in scope. Some such groups ought to be within the knowledge of every well-informed minister. World news in the press, world magazines, and world broadcasts over the radio have helped to make this easier in recent years. He who follows a world leader must be a world citizen. That necessitates knowledge of world groups and forces. Otherwise localism and provincialism hold sway and the world service program of any church fades out, or undue dependence is placed on the judgment of distant "experts." Instead such a program needs to be intelligently and democratically worked out at home in co-operation with denominational plans.

The minister, therefore, must know groups extensively— all sorts and kinds of people, in all sorts and kinds of groups. He will never permit himself that strange quirk of evasion indulged by some ministers who pride themselves on their ignorance of "this world." He will rather aspire to share effectively in creative group relationships in a democracy.

About groups intensively, inner processes and efficiency factors. An intensive knowledge of group processes is also greatly to be desired. But even the social psychologists and the experts in "group work" have not yet arrived at many conclusions about the laws and principles that govern group processes. It is an area of human association in which the relative unpredictability of the personal factor bulks large. What succeeds in one group with one leader may not succeed in the same group with another leader nor with the same leader in another group. The attitudes of some leaders, coercive, dictatorial, authoritative, and instructional, or of others, friendly, eliciting, democratic, and receptive of ideas, are also highly important. The purposes of members—both the stated purposes and the actual but often concealed purposes—are other important variables. Suitable settings and equipment that facilitate group solidarity are likewise influential.

Ministers must discover if they can how attitudes and processes differ as between men's groups and women's groups or mixed groups; what processes succeed at one age level but not at another, how wide a diversity in types of persons strongly holding variant convictions can be included without the sacrifice of spiritual cohesion, the ways in which divisive ethical issues can be handled and group unity yet be maintained, how to break up the mental inertia of some members and get them to thinking without in the least determining what they shall think. He will want to know how processions with bands, banners, and badges affect group loyalties. He will ask how large a group for discussion may be without loss of unity. Such a conclusion as the Friends are said to have reached on this point is suggestive: that sixty persons is about as many as can fully share creatively in one of their meetings. He will study the procedures by which a skillful leader guides the exploration of an issue which has not yet been thought out by the group members, how he can secure freedom of participation and also a sequence of thought toward a group conclusion. How can a leader guide the group process so that individualistic attitudes become constructive and the spirit harmonious rather than divisive? How develop group morale and replace low standards with higher ones? These and similar questions need searching study by ministers. There are no patent answers. A minister's success or failure may depend in large measure upon his skill in group processes and his ability to train effective leaders of voluntary groups.

JESUS AND GROUPS

Jesus was shaped by groups. It is implicit in the records of His life and teaching that He was profoundly influenced by groups. No lack of a chronological account of His group experiences need blind us to the internal evidence. We cite but two illustrations, a positive influence and a negative.

First the family group—a loving father in the background, a meditative, realizing mother in the foreground, numerous brothers and sisters about—a typical Jewish family. The children were evidently reared with care, the ritual requirements fulfilled. They were students of the Scriptures. They worked daily in the home, in the carpenter shop, and upon the soil. They were in touch with other family and village groups. Such a family furnished the early settings of His life and provided the structural basis for His thought. The gigantic figures He flung upon the sky were family figures: God the benign parent, strong like a father, tender like a mother; the vast company of all men and women, His brothers and sisters, all within the innumerable family of God. His whole teaching, essentially so simple, is a revelation of the depth of family influence upon Him. His teaching is universally understandable because of the universal presence of families of some sort in all human experience. Other groups influenced Him positively but the family most profoundly and familiarly so.

Jesus was also influenced negatively, by a mixed group in Jerusalem which He branded as "scribes and Pharisees, hypocrites." They were meticulous about the Jewish law and their own fine-spun interpretations of it, about ritual requirements which no ordinary man could comply with, about separation of Jews as superior persons from inferior Gentiles. They were prize exhibitionists, conspicious in all public places, ostentatiously greeting each other. They were outwardly concerned about pious observances but really concerned about their power over people—power for their own ends—so that, in cahoots with lawyers of a certain stripe, as the custom is with cowards, they might lay intolerable burdens upon ordinary men and themselves not have to touch one of the burdens, not even with a little finger. He seems early to have recognized this group as the complete embodiment of opposition to everything He stood for. Their influence upon Him was evidently profound, for they had power to block His message with the people. That which blocked his message vitally affected Him. Steadily He grew in the realization of the irreconcilable issue between them. This must have intensified the concern that drove Him into solitude, led Him to renewed meditation and prayer and to secret conferences with the twelve. His acute sensitivity in relationships took Him straight to the center of the perfidy of the hypocrites and heightened the beauty of his vision of unselfish love. Could any antitheses be sharper? Legalism stood against spiritual liberty, meticulosity in ritual detail against human freedom, separatism against inclusive love, vanity against humility, the cruel against the tender, the venal against the spiritual, petty little advantages for today against eternal values, self against God.

The nature of the process by which Jesus arrived at His unique message to humanity lies hidden behind the veil, but suggestive clues are visible. Could it be that He got His message or clarified it by a deep realization of opposites, since these men and their ideas, their attitudes and practices were the logical antitheses of His own? Coming into contact with them early in His life as He did, and recurrently afterward, could it be that He arrived at His very ideas of rightness in relationships, as by white against black, in contrast to theirs? True greatness in persons, as He grew to conceive it, was in exact and diametrical opposition to their cruel pettiness. All this was manifestly one of the deepening and anguishing realizations of His life—to find such a gang ensconced in the holy Temple of His ancestral faith, in absolute control of Jerusalem, exploiting the people whom He loved, subverting by trickery the very law about which they prated. So the conviction grew, the inevitable issue intensified, and "from that time began Jesus to show unto his disciples, that He must go unto Jerusalem, and suffer many things of the elders and chief priests and scribes." Since Jesus knew persons in groups as well as individually, He knew that this gangster lot would stop at nothing. He knew they were the power group of His nation. He knew full well that they had the power, as indeed they later proved, but He moved on undaunted. They lay in wait to catch Him on legal technicalities. They followed Him all about, snooping and spying on Him, contradicting Him before His listeners, asking Him all manner of catch-questions, and trying to stir up the people against Him. They lied about Him, bribed one of His own inner group, and condemned Him in direct contravention of their own law. They intimidated the Roman governor, used the mob to clinch the final action, and then having achieved His crucifixion they mocked Him as He died in anguish, scoffing at Him and wagging their vindicative old heads. Then afterwards the cowards got a Roman guard and sealed up His tomb, so great was their fear of His mysterious power. "Whited sepulchres," "serpents, offspring of vipers"—He had known them of old. And yet even of them He said, "Father, forgive them, for they know not what they do."

His final triumph over death and over all the death-dealing powers by which they won their victory makes it easy to forget the power of their influence over Him. This is visible not alone in the tragic last events, not alone in the hateful qualities they embodied—negatives for His positives—but in His calm facing of all the facts of destiny involved, in the sheer daring and triumphant courage with which He moved into the very centers of their deadly hate. It is more than an illustration of group influence upon Him. It is the everlasting epitome of the spiritual triumph of one lone fighter for the right over the bitter hostility of a power group. More than one scarred fighter for social justice today secretly loves Him for this though he may not openly give allegiance.

Jesus used groups. He was not only influenced profoundly by groups; He used them. Jesus used two people as a group again and again to carry His messages. "And when they drew nigh unto Jerusalem, and came unto Bethphage unto the mount of Olives, then Jesus sent two disciples, saying." "And He calleth unto Him the twelve, and began to send them forth by two and two." He was evidently well aware of the strength of a two-group, especially when united for high ends. In the light of our thinking about groups a fresh significance attaches to these words, "Again I say unto you, that if two of you shall agree on earth as touching anything that they shall ask, it shall be done for them of my Father who is in heaven. For where two or three are gathered together in my name, there am I in the midst of them." Do you suppose He might have had in mind a husband and wife with a little child or a guest praying together?

So also He used the seventy unit, not for an audience as we would do, but as messengers to go forth two by two. Seventy in Jewish thought was the right number for any important piece of public work. "After these things the Lord appointed seventy others, and sent them two and two before his face into every city and place, whither He himself was about to come." Later on, the seventy returned with joy to report to Him, evidently to be recommissioned and sent out again after a period of reflection and group refreshment in His presence.

Jesus' chief use of a group was of course in the twelve. Twelve was the number He fixed on. He quite definitely chose them out from the larger number of His disciples. They are referred to some thirty-four times as "the twelve" in the four Gospels and the book of Acts. Jesus seems to have fixed upon the number twelve for social efficiency's sake rather than because of the number's significance in Hebrew history. Large enough to give diversity, small enough to make for unity, not too difficult to harmonize, twelve has repeatedly demonstrated itself as a highly workable unit for group thought and action.

The personnel of the twelve is significant from the angle of our interest in all sorts and kinds of persons.

The apostles without exception belonged to the working classes as they would be called today. There was no man of rank or distinction or of social consideration among them. Four of them, we know, were fishermen. One of them was a collector of taxes. The rest belonged to the same rank in life, and followed similar occupations. All of them knew what it was to labor to maintain themselves; they were familiar with life as it presents itself to the great body of mankind. There is no evidence that any of the Apostles were specially distinguished by intellectual force. There was no man of genius among them; no original thinker; no man dowered with the imaginative faculty; no man of great powers of organization. It does not appear that any of them had an unusually impressive or attractive personality. As far as can be ascertained, they were all young men, about the same age as, or younger than, our Lord Himself. No man of middle life, no gray head was included in the circle. Variety of taste, temper, mode of life found full expression among the Apostles. No one was the same as another. Their experience of life had differed. Their anticipation of the future differed. Their habits of thought and action differed. Perhaps the only common elements were their piety and their devotion to Jesus. Such then were the Apostles. They were pious men belonging to the people, full of the plain sense and judgment that mark the common man: slow to learn but teachable; free from social prejudices; untrammelled by any fixed system of thought; with keen eyes for character; anxious to win the favor of Jesus.[1]

At two points His purpose in the use of the twelve-group is given. Once was in the second period of the Galilean ministry when "He appointed twelve of them, whom he called apostles, to be with Him and to be sent out to preach, with power to drive out the demons."[2] But there was a larger purpose, a wider scope for which He had selected them, sent them forth, trained them, had them report back to Him, recommitted His message to them, gone with them to solitary places for refreshment, and taken them with Him up to Jerusalem that they might share His suffering. The purpose of all this breathes through the fourteenth, fifteenth, sixteenth, and seventeenth chapters of the Gospel of St. John—the best loved passages in the whole sweep of historic literature. In the first chapter of the Acts of the Apostles He is said to have epitomized His purpose for them in these words: "You will be witnesses for me in Jerusalem and all over Judea and Samaria and to the very ends of the earth."[3]

Jesus created an enduring spiritual fellowship. "To the very ends of the earth!" With a wistful vagueness that little phrase is tacked on to complete the extension throughout the

---

[1] William Patrick, "Apostles," in *A Dictionary of Christ and the Gospels,* Charles Scribner's Sons, New York, 1907.

[2] Mark 3:14. Goodspeed translation.

[3] Acts 1:8. Goodspeed translation.

then known world. It is a fresh clue to His inclusiveness. The utterance of that phrase is the point of transition from the face-to-face group of His immediate followers out to the Church Invisible—the enduring fellowship of all those who name His name and share His purposes. That vast inclusive fellowship is truly a group, though in a different sense from the twelve. From the spiritual creativity He quickened in the twelve the Church Invisible has come forth by geometrical progression till it has become a spiritual fellowship no man can number, yet still includes face-to-face groups the world around. The faith of Jesus that such a multitude of groups of persons would, through the centuries, name His name has been validated by the event.

Who are the true kindred of Christ in all times and everywhere? Who really belong in His fellowship? "While He was still speaking, His mother and His brothers came up and stood outside the crowd, wanting to speak to Him. But He said to the man who told him, 'Who is my mother, and who are my brothers?' And He pointed to His disciples and said, 'Here are my mother and my brothers! For whoever does the will of my Father in heaven is my brother and sister and mother!' " [4]

How, then, shall one rightly think of His Church save as a universal spiritual fellowship? How shall one think of any particular church save as a worshiping group whose members rejoice to witness to one another and to the world in word and deed about Jesus? The Christian Church is both an invisible fellowship and a multitude of visible voluntary groups. It is as simple and as profound as that. With just enough organization between the groups to carry out His purposes, church groups require no elaborate ecclesiastical structure, no central bureaucracy or official hierarchy. Rather do they

[4] Matthew 12:46-50. Goodspeed translation.

live by the rediscovery of Jesus in their own creative fellowship. This, of course, is only one interpretation of the Church; but to many this seems the interpretation nearest to the Church of the first century, the most democratic, the most enduring, the one which most emphasizes creative groups.

There is perennial need for quickening and guidance on the part of all such groups. That is a major ministerial function, since there are so many church groups lacking in vitality of life and thought, in commitment to His purposes, in any generous sharing with needy people, and in any Christian world consciousness. Shall the Church invisible live forever? That depends largely on whether enough witnessing groups still shall continue to abide in the earth and perennially recreate themselves anew. That will require abundance of life in the persons who comprise such groups and the same commitment as that which led Him to the Cross and to the creation of His vast fellowship.

A MINISTER HEIGHTENS HIS SKILLS WITH GROUPS

In the light of Jesus' use of groups, ministers who face the facts of group influence in themselves, in their parishes, their communities, and beyond, will often be baffled as to the part they as individuals can play. It is a far cry from the many vicious, exploitive groups of any American region to an adequate number of fellowship groups of the followers of Jesus. But in that wide gap lies the very strain and tension out of which comes the power of creative religious effort. Ministers who realize the subversive group influences which impinge upon their people in contrast to His purposes for them are forced to form creative groups to match and master these evil forces. They must first be quickeners themselves, quickened from within.

How shall a minister quicken groups? The basic answer lies, of course, in the quality of the person. Is there about a minister a kindling quality caught from Jesus? Is there a downright beauty, a rightness, and an outreach which sets other persons aflame? If these qualities of livingness and love are in him, he will be perforce a quickener and a leader of groups. His methods will work themselves out, under God, by His own commitment, by his own initiative, and by intelligent study of the laws of leadership. The results as shown in his attitudes and methods will largely determine his success or failure in his ministry to groups and through groups.

But how? The following points are suggested:

The minister fully accepts the voluntary principle. First he will acknowledge and live by the voluntary principle, for wherever external coercions are in control of groups, creative religion departs. His problems in relationships will ease up almost immediately when he eliminates from himself every vestige of coercive method and all command psychology and substitutes the methods of winsomeness. Shall he fail to let others exercise the liberty that is in Jesus? Shall he fail to help them use that liberty habitually to creative ends? Shall a Christian give up his freedom and come again into bondage to autocracy? Must we not all maintain at all costs freedom from all compulsion in religious faith and practice in America? This is the foundation stone of our democracy as solidly set in our history as Plymouth Rock itself. "For this our exiled fathers crossed the seas," and for our freedom from any brand of coercive state religion we may well continue to be grateful. Compulsion in religious faith or practices is always dangerous. Compulsory attendance of young people at religious exercises or compulsory membership in religious groups is often a disservice to religion and is sometimes indeed an incitement to rebellion. If ministers cannot learn how to compete with the world by the winsomeness of the message they have for men they had better not take the dangerous short cuts of compulsion. Fortunately our American democratic spirit naturally expresses itself in voluntary groupings. Happy is the minister who neither wants nor will tolerate any authoritative coercions to be used on his behalf, who rejoices to deal with voluntary groups which he has to win. That is one of the priceless assets of our American Protestant tradition and is to be treasured for what it is, even though it seems to make the minister's task more difficult. Like it or not, we are compelled to accept the terms of the game as they are. We deal with voluntary groups in contrast to state or hierarchical agencies.

Furthermore, the minister does well to treasure voluntary groups in face of the standardizing of our present cultural patterns. Our commercial amusements, for example, are breaking down selective groupings and forcing the young people into miscellaneous and heterogeneous audience-crowds. Realize the meaning of that! The regimentation by profit-seekers of this most freedom-loving element in all our life— our play—is the precise way to crush the spontaneity of the amateur spirit and to create the mob mind. Our commercial amusements are already as standardized as automobile parts. Block booking is symbolic. A discerning sociologist recently said, "The most devastating thing in American life today is the destruction of our cultural patterns in small voluntary groups." That, by the way, is the real tragedy in the break-up of the Sabbath in urban life. The passing over of family groups, of friendship groups, and of congregations into purposeless crowds and disconnected masses implies the subjection of our people to many kinds of social pressures. But from all regimentation they are beginning to turn away to intimate friendly groups for a deepened "sense of belonging," for a fresh security in a free society.

The person-minded minister does well to realize in his own life also the meaning of voluntarism. No external compulsion drafted him into the ministry of Christ. And Jesus

Himself chose. His is the great example. Compulsion was, is, and must be from within.

> It is not martyrdom to toss
> In anguish on the deadly cross:
> But to have will'd to perish so,
> To will it through each bodily throe,
> To will it with still-tortured mind
> This, only this, redeems mankind.[5]

To give up the voluntary in religion is to revert to externalism, to authoritarianism, to militarism. There you are again, before you know it, at the bottom of the old slippery slide of brow-beating, coercions, hostilities, and war. One of the surest signs of essential weakness in any minister, parent, group leader, teacher, executive, or bishop is to become autocratic. To have to resort to coercions based on fear compulsion demonstrates a lack of sufficient skill in creative relationships to win the loyalty necessary for team play and the triumph of team or family or church. In any religious group Christianity is betrayed in the house of its friends unless the voluntary choices, the inner disciplines, are in control.

It is a high art, a difficult task to win children, young people, and older people to the voluntary choice of the best in life, but person-minded ministers of Christ rejoice in that alternative. Only the mysterious inner forces within persons and groups grow, first the blade, then the ear, then the full corn in the ear. These are not the patterns of growth in big business or bureaucracies, but are the processes with which person-minded ministers are concerned. When some of the present regimentations of American life have been thrown off, voluntarism will come into its own again—is already doing so.

The minister quickens groups around interests of his own.

[5] Henrik Ibsen, *Brand*.

How? This is not as difficult as it seems to some ministers who are afraid to be their natural selves with their people. Take it on a point of easy pick-up. Every healthy man is interested in something out of doors, baseball, hiking, camping, photography, swimming, fishing, hunting, or in some indoor things like furniture making, stamp collecting, music, games, radio, amateur movies, discussion of public questions, or some favorite type of reading. He may gather about himself a little group or groups to share his interests. Many of the finest human relationships grow up around an enthusiasm shared thus with others in a small informal company, a scout troop, a camping party, a reading club. Many a minister, sharing his hobbies without conscious effort, is already deepening his friendships. A bit of careful thought about his people would reveal new possibilities for wider friendships to be born by socializing his own personal interests. Valuable though such groups may be, they are of course but means to ends. They are limited by personal interests.

The minister quickens groups around the interests of others. A more objective basis can be found in a study of the major interests of the people in his parish and the quickening of groups about them. A bit of social analysis helps greatly at this point. Many such groups are of course already in existence, though often unrecognized because they are informal or ephemeral. Some of these interests in addition to religious interests in the narrower sense, are being served by some churches. Among them are the universal interest in play, which too many churches have neglected; interest in occupations, such as milk production, mining, grain farming, cotton growing, factory work, merchandizing, or government service. These vital interests the churches have, on the whole, treated skittishly. Besides these are the relations of men and women before marriage and in marriage, the responsibilities of fatherhood and motherhood, the care and rearing of children. Such interests were at the very center of Jesus' thinking. One suspects that a young married couple's club, a mother's friendly circle, or a father's group would suit His mind. Choice of a vocation and finding employment are responsibilities that frighten many young people today, yet urge them on. Making a living and making a home are twin companions. When these are thwarted both natural development and marriage are interrupted. But any alert minister will find in these fundamental interests of his people spontaneous eruption points at which informal groups might readily be formed. In short-time or long-time groups the interests of other persons may be socialized and interpreted in the light of Jesus' teaching.

The minister quickens groups around the purposes of Jesus. More deeply imbedded still in the essential nature of a Christian fellowship are Jesus' purposes for rightness and social outreach in persons. His call for the establishment of the realm of love swings any person-minded man or woman away out beyond the orbits of his limited personal interests or those of his neighbors, yet not away from them. To share in the meeting of human need in the light of the ideals of the Kingdom is to quicken creative groups upon the highest levels. His purposes, as we know, included the bringing of good news to poor people, release to prisoners, sight to the blind, and liberty to the downtrodden. To quicken new groups or to impregnate existing groups with His purposes is the most essential service of a person-minded minister in dealing with groups. He may achieve this by choirs and choral music, by spiritual harmony in worship, by religious drama, by effective teaching in religious education, by courageous community action in facing social problems. He and his people may share in groups for the clearance of slum areas and for aiding settlements, hospitals, and clinics, in interracial conferences, in courageous group work for just conditions of labor, in groups opposing war. For these and many other great causes

do men and women now work in groups in the spirit of
Jesus. They help to bring in the day when His purposes,
finally shared by innumerable voluntary groups, shall at last
prevail.

A particular church is not to be thought of, therefore, as a
static organization cumbered with hostages to this world, full
of rigid attitudes and procedures which wreck the free flow
of spiritual impulses, an ecclesiastical institution over which
the minister presides as a sort of manager under the control
of "ruling elders." It is rather to be thought of as a living,
democratic fellowship of persons, each concerned for all and
all for each, a center where interacting groups of persons think
and work, worship and pray freely to the end that the purposes of Jesus may be fulfilled through them. Quickened by
their ministers, many living churches are such fellowships.

The minister guides groups. Ministers are little recognized
as social engineers, but engineers they must in some sense be
if they are to be effective guides of group thought and action.
Groups require more than quickening and organizing, more
than liberating from inertia and rigidity. Some have had their
day yet have not ceased to be. They need anaesthesia. Others
have become ends in themselves, are being kept alive for the
sake of official positions to be occupied by persons ambitious
for personal distinction. They need nothing so much as pain-
less extinction. Group structures in and of themselves have no
more sanctity than do other means of doing work. The tests
are always in the services rendered to persons who are seeking
the good, the beautiful, the true, or who need so to seek.

Even the best of groups need guidance—constant guidance
from the Eternal Source of Wisdom, guidance also from wise
leaders, of whom the minister should be one. Some groups
need to be set going and left free to run themselves. Some
need a weekly bath and check-up. Some need group training
and discipline. Some need frank speech about inner trends,

honest facing of such trends, and a widening of purposes. Some need enlarging, others contracting. Some need the gospel of self help, others to foster mutual aid and co-operative processes. Some need galvanizing with new blood, especially young blood. Others are carrying too much sail, lack ballast, and are sure to keel over in a gust of wind. Some are broken in their morale by the domination of little bosses and autocrats who have outlived their usefulness as officers but do not know it; the tenure of such officers needs the gentle corrective of a democratic terminal procedure. Some groups haven't had a new idea since the memory of the oldest member knoweth not when. They might get a new one if they got a new president and a new executive committee or if, when a prophetic voice was heard in their midst, they were elastic enough to follow it in a courageous new project.

He is a wise minister who learns for himself, as he must, how to fulfill his function as a guide of voluntary groups and to heighten them to Christian levels. This he must do with a wise head, a patient hand, a low voice, and temper well controlled. And then he must, if he can, come off unembittered by criticisms, misunderstandings, and misinterpretations, undaunted by his own mistakes. Any skillful guide of church groups or those of similar type will have to face some very ornery facts about persons, realize the meanings of such facts, aid in doing what can be done to correct them with individual members as well as with the groups themselves. He will seek to set both persons and groups forward in the great quests of life. If he should succeed in this he will be a skillful minister indeed.

One draws back to look at the spectacle of groups in American life. One sees the multiplicity of them, ruminates a bit on our humorous propensity to overdo them, realizes the short-lived futility of many of them and the extraordinary power to multiply spiritual values shown by others. One then asks oneself: "Where does all this come out? What is accomplished? Are groups ends in themselves?" In answering, we first lay aside the vicious, criminal, and exploitative groups as subversive, as neither ends nor means to worthwhile values. But much confusion as to means and ends persists in groups originally creative and constructive, especially in certain well-established ones which have constitutions, property, paraphernalia, and traditions. Such groups easily ossify into institutions. The purposes of the founders are often forgotten or distorted by specious interpretations of indispensability. Many an institution becomes an end in itself. Loyalty coalesces about it; men and women live, work, and die for it. Reputation is established in it and by it. New members then come in for the sake of prestige and other personal advantages. Old members stick around and find their security in it. The elders are honored as founders. The stiffening process deepens. Rigor mortis finally sets in. Unless endowed, the property may be sold to pay off the mortgages. The obsequies are in the silent soliloquies of a few old men. Many a creative beginning has had an ending like that! Many a living group has degenerated into an institution, has become an end in itself, and has died of institutional arterio-sclerosis. The plain truth is that more than one well-endowed old wealthy urban church has stiffened down like that. Meantime the essential purposes of the founders are being excellently carried out in obscure but courageous poverty by little groups of young persons just around the corner. No critical generalizations about institutions as such are here intended, but the tendencies described are actual in many groups and suggest some of the dangers involved when groups become ends in themsleves.

Some churches seem prone to such dangers, particularly when many members think or say: "There is little we feel impelled to witness about Jesus. As a matter of fact, we rarely mention Him. We let the preacher do it for us on Sundays at eleven. It is easy for us to repeat and to sing—especially to sing—what nobody expects us to prove we mean. We find it easy to enjoy other people's fine purposes without making them our own. It is socially suitable for us to be church members. It puts us in with the people who count. It is easy to listen to an eloquent sermon if we don't have to change anything anywhere." Such attitudes are sure symptoms of hardening of the arteries. A witnessing fellowship is no longer there. Only husks are left. It is no light matter to ask a young man to match his growing life to a dead thing like that. Could Jesus' words about a dead father apply to a dead church also? "Follow me and let the dead bury their dead." Possibly one little inner circle of two or three members praying and living creatively might bring it back to life. Such a thing has been known to happen.

GROUP RESULTS ARE IN PERSONS

The ends of Christian groups are in persons rather than in the groups themselves. Even the best institutions are instruments not ends. It is the people who are important. Groups, especially Christian groups, are for the sake of persons. They are to aid persons to become different persons, to give them a sense of togetherness, to train them in social attitudes and practices, to teach them thoughtfulness for one another, to keep them from sagging down into selfishness, to carry on the priceless messages of Jesus. They may thus become persons of deepest honesty, filled with concern for each other, for all other persons and human needs. Such persons are the true products of true churches. Such results in persons come, however, only from basic and persistent loyalty to the purposes of Jesus and above all from loyalty to Himself. Such persons in such groups led by person-minded ministers, living in creative relationships, have in themselves the power to recreate society, and to bring in the realm of love.

VIII

THE MINISTER AS CREATIVE PART-NER IN A NEW SOCIAL ORDER

PERSONS ARE SOCIAL PRODUCTS

IT is now manifest that persons are largely social products. The forces that shape a human life arise in part from native abilities, personal experiences, and habits; but even the most individualistic elements are seen, upon analysis, to be profoundly affected by influences coming from other persons and from society at large. Physical settings in childhood—New York tenement or Ozark mountain cabin—mark a boy deeply. Economic conditions—wealth or poverty—determine much. Social customs, social institutions and current beliefs about life are inescapable influences. Persons growing up in England, China, Russia or America are inevitably different, even if basic racial differences are ignored. Americans are American social products, branded by prevalent conditions, customs, institutions, standards, and beliefs—obviously so—but the implications run deep and far.

All loyal Americans rejoice in American standards of living, literacy, and public education; also in our traditions of political liberty and representative government. The "hundred-per-centers," being grateful that we have come as far as we have, look upon conditions here as the best possible. They want us all to take it easy where we are, to rest content with the status quo. Not so our searchers! We yield to no man in gratitude that we have come as far as we have, nor in loyalty to the finest American traditions and ideals. American ideals have been powerful shapers of the American people from the brave beginnings in colonial days, and still make us tighten our belts to push on to a juster order of society even here—especially here—because of the courage which has already been displayed in our history, and because of our unique responsibility in the midst of world bewilderment.

FOUR APPROACHES TO AMERICAN SOCIAL PROBLEMS

Realistic minds have a habit of facing facts. They want the truth, the whole truth, and nothing but the truth. They don't like to be fooled, nor to fool themselves. They are particularly careful, therefore, to put the spotlight and the microscope upon the social danger points, social diseases, and the public enemies, just as a thorough diagnostician relentlessly hunts down the presence of cancer or tuberculosis.

The author's approaches to these issues in American life, extending through many years, have been four. They are suggested here neither as ideal nor as complete and yet as offering four types of inquiry which, among others, are worthy the consideration of ministers.

First-hand contacts with urban congestion and rural problems. These approaches originated in first-hand experiences during college years with underprivileged boys and with broken men in the congested areas of New Haven, Connecticut. Later, as an assistant minister of a downtown church in New York City, he had the pastoral care of families ranging from Fifth Avenue to the Hudson river, and went back and forth through city streets from the homes of the well-to-do to tenement rooms of tragic poverty. There the contrasts between wealth and poverty burn themselves into one's consciousness. At one end are women in their limousines, decorated with enough orchids—the playthings of an afternoon—to supply food for a week to a poverty-stricken family in abject need living not three blocks away. Thousands upon thousands of people travel uptown and downtown through these areas daily. Few, however, go crosstown with their sociological eyes open to the epitome of economic contrasts presented there.

Later on, over a period of six summers, the author brought students to New York City from widespread colleges and universities and plunged them into those same contrasts in various sections of the city. They were attached to churches, settlements, and Christian Associations in order that they might have at least a taste of first-hand experience in grappling with such conditions under the guidance of Christian leaders representing different viewpoints. This "New York College Summer Service Group" has continued to give students similar experiences every summer for twenty-four years and has brought nearly a thousand of them to sharp realization of social problems thereby.

A similar approach to rural conditions has been made with students of Cornell University over a period of years by means of student deputations to nearby towns and villages in central New York state, and in conferences with local pastors. This approach has been widened in the last four years through "The Lisle Fellowship," under the leadership of the Reverend and Mrs. Dewitt Baldwin, returned missionaries from Burma, acting interdenominationally under the Methodist Board of Foreign Missions. Some two hundred students in four summers have come from widespread colleges and universities to Lisle for summer periods of six weeks. These have included forty nationals from twelve different countries, representatives of twenty denominations and four religions other than Christianity. One hundred and eighty-seven deputation teams have visited more than a hundred communities within a radius of one hundred miles. Intensive training has been given these students for facing local problems in rural, mining, and factory communities in New York State and northern Pennsylvania. Christian interracial relations and world-mindedness have been demonstrated in this Fellowship. In it and in the New York City group the emphases have been upon fact-getting, deeper understanding of human needs, shared living, and the power of Christian principles to solve social problems. The honest discussion and presentation of these principles by students has deeply influenced both them and the persons with whom they have shared their developing thought and life.

These first-hand approaches to social problems with students have been kept free from doctrinaire propaganda, have been democratic in method and Christian in motivation. They have yielded creative changes both in social relationships and in life purposes.

The systematic study of American social conditions. The second main approach was a systematic study of American social conditions shared with students and others at the University of Wisconsin through the organization of "Social Problems Groups." The first of these met at the First Congregational Church in Madison, Wisconsin, in 1905, under the guidance of Prof. E. A. Ross, Prof. John Commons, Miss Jane Addams, Miss Mary McDowell, Mr. Louis F. Post, Mr. and Mrs. Raymond Robins, and others. Open discussion based on fact-finding characterized this approach, but with no propaganda for any particular solutional answer save a deep belief in Christian principles and in creative Christian living as applied to these problems. Each of the following problems was analyzed as to major facts involved, leading proposals looking toward solutions, and the application of Christian principles:

(1) The Liquor Problem, (2) The Race Problem, (3) The Labor Problem, (4) Immigration, (5) Poverty, (6) Concentrated Wealth, (7) Marital Problems, (8) Juvenile Delinquency, (9) The Increase in Crime and the Administration of Criminal Justice, (10) The Treatment of Criminals, (11)

Popular Amusements, (12) Prevalent Business Morals, (13) Public Health and Sanitation, (14) Municipal Government, (15) The Social Role of the Churches, (16) The Conservation of Natural Resources, (17) The Problems of Rural Life, (18) The Problems of American Women, (19) The Problem of Organized Vice, (20) The Malformation of Public Opinion, (21) The Control of Public Utilities, (22) International Problems—War.

That approach continues to be sound. Every one of these problems is still urgent in American life and calls for solution by direct study and intelligent social action. If during the last thirty-five years large numbers of groups of Christian men and women in American churches, colleges, and universities had been wrestling with the issues involved in such problems by an inductive procedure, without doctrinaire propaganda, a vast body of Christian public opinion might have been democratically developed.

First-hand studies of local community life. The third approach is that of "Christianizing community life." [1] The purpose here has been for socially minded Christians to take a particular American community set in the wide background of world community life; to see in it the family as the indispensable social unit, and the social injustices that take their toll from family life; to study the needs of children—all children in that community; to study the basic necessity for the education of young and old alike for social living; to give special heed to the problems of the weak, the poverty-stricken, the sick, the juvenile delinquents, and the underworld weaklings; to face the exploitations of labor, especially the age-old injustices of child labor, the working conditions of women, seasonal unemployment, and the lot of migrant laborers; to

[1] Harry F. Ward and Richard Henry Edwards, *Christianizing Community Life*, Association Press, New York, 1918.

match the principles of political democracy to present auto-cratic systems of industrial management and along with these the Christian ideals of industrial democracy; to study the inequitable administration of justice as between rich and poor, colored and white, political insiders and common men who have no special influence; to dare to search out and face the invisible government behind the governmental fronts in any American city; to know who are the public enemies, the grafters, the racketeers, and the exploiters; to face in the very institutions of religion an undemocratic and unchristian con-trol by men of wealth and power wherever they occur; and finally to attempt to visualize a truly Christian community as a sample of the Christian social order.

That also is a sound approach—an American approach.

First-hand studies of areas of special need. The fourth approach is to focus upon areas of need and human misery in special regional groups, such as the victims of drought in the dust bowl, flood victims in the lowlands of the river valleys, migrant workers, sharecroppers, and wage hands of tobacco and cotton producing areas, soft coal miners, swamp dwellers of the large river deltas, Southern mountaineers, mill workers in the worst of the factory towns, Cajan groups of Louisiana and Alabama, and stranded peoples in once prosperous com-munities from which industries have moved away without regard for the human factor. There are often in such groups and areas tragic needs involving human misery for vast num-bers of persons. Such conditions are now seen as national rather than local or regional problems. Government aid, Red Cross, and similar help have brought great relief to many areas and stricken groups. Such areas of suffering, however, put upon churches and ministers responsibility for aggressive initiative in facing the injustices of the present social order. The arousal of the churches for social action which shall be democratic in method and Christian in character and motivation is clearly required.

We cite an encouraging example out of recent experience, that of a group of fifty Arkansas Methodist ministers who have been making special studies during 1937, 1938, and 1939 of the problems of life and labor as affected by land tenancy in that state. This has involved a searching review of the sharecropper and wage-hand problems in cotton producing communities based on the intimate knowledge of ministers working in them. The author has acted as secretary to this group. As in other approaches cited, this inquiry has been made by the establishment of mutual confidence among the types of persons concerned, without negative prejudgments, personal biases, or propaganda for any particular solution of the problems involved. Four points have been kept steadily in view: (1) What are the actual facts and what is their human meaning? (2) What are the most hopeful measures now being taken to improve conditions? (3) What do the principles of Jesus require of His followers in such difficult relationships? (4) What more can be done by ministers and church groups to improve these conditions and relationships?

This approach conducted with searching honesty and great frankness by these ministers themselves has brought to us all as participant searchers a deep realization of the human tragedy involved for thousands of persons in cotton producing areas. It has brought better understanding of the complexities of the elements that enter into this problem. Deep conviction has come to us that direct constructive action in the spirit of intelligent love must be taken by Christians in their local and regional life, likewise that national contributions must be made.

Once again we come to believe in a multiple solution with many groups and agencies contributing. This, however, in no way delays a group of ministers in formulating programs for local action or courageously working out such programs in any region. This experience of a regional social study by a selected group of ministers illustrates, indeed, a sound, democratic, Christian approach to any set of aggravated conditions and relationships in any area. What any group of ministers and their people will achieve in such a situation will depend upon their own realistic courage, as criticism and opposition are sure to arise. The answer will be found in the event alone.

There are, of course, many other urgently needed approaches. These four are but samples, somewhat tried and tested in the author's own experience. They can therefore be honestly suggested in these meditations.

Twenty years ago Lord Bryce wrote the Master of Balliol College, Oxford, these words which emphasize the urgency of social studies:

> 8 Buckingham Gate
> London, S. W. 1
> March 14, 1919

My Dear Master:

In my judgment there has never been a time at which the systematic and impartial study of social and economic questions has been so urgent as at the present day. We stand on the threshold of a new age. The problems which confront us and the other leading democratic states of the world are of the most complex and the most vital character, and can only be solved by patient examination conducted in a spirit of scientific detachment, accompanied by a wide diffusion of adult civic education. To avert grave conflicts between classes and interests we must in good time enquire into and determine so far as possible their causes and conditions. We need, therefore, today and at once a much more adequate provision for social research and for giving publicity to the results of such research. But to be most fruitful our work must be conceived in a large and liberal spirit. No country lives to itself in these times. In particular, the experience in economic and social development which has been obtained in the British

Self-Governing Dominions and in the United States of America, carefully recorded and commented on, is of the greatest value. . . . .

I am,

Sincerely yours,

BRYCE

MINISTERS MUST SUFFER WITH SUFFERING PERSONS

"What business has a minister with these great social evils? Why should he concern himself about them? Why should he not stick to individual persons and to voluntary groups and leave society and all the world's great problems to those who know more about them? "Cobbler, stick to your last." So runs the argument. We had better thresh out that question in these meditations.

We rejoin by asking: what, then, is the cobbler's last? That question raises antecedent issues. Is or is not the gospel a universal gospel? Are all men, women, and children sacred, or only a few? Are Christians obligated to transform our whole present-day society into a Christian social order? The undodgeable issue confronting modern Christianity, as we see it, lies in these questions. The most discerning socially minded young people say flatly today that the future of the Christian Church depends upon how it meets this issue. The convictions of such young people are not to be ignored, for in them lies the potential leadership of tomorrow.

Our thesis is that social problems are a fundamental and inescapable concern of the Christian minister. That is chiefly for three reasons:

Evil forces are at work in every community. This first reason for a minister's concern is an immediate and practical one. These evils cut right into the lives of the individuals and groups to whom he is devoting his life. He could not escape them if he would. When the father of a high school girl comes in and tells him in the confessional that his daughter has been infected with gonorrhea, the minister had better believe that social diseases are some of his business. When a young widow in his parish cannot get work, drags along half starved through months of discouragement, and then suddenly goes off to New York to live the kind of life that is there so easily possible, the whole dastardly business of the exploitation of women by men becomes inescapably some of the minister's business. He cannot escape responsibility if he would—any more than a farmer can ignore worms in his apple trees, or rust in his wheat, or flood wreckage on his lowland meadow; any more than a mother can refuse to recognize the presence of diseases that infect her children right out of the air they breathe. When people in his parish, dairy farmers, can't get enough out of the New York milk distributor's pot to clothe their children decently and give them medical care when they are sick, the economics of New York State milk distribution is inescapably some of his business. If he lives in the bootleg coal area of Pennsylvania where great mines of anthracite coal have been closed down by absentee owners who won't make any move to solve unemployment, then the economics of the coal mining industry in America is right down his alley. He could not escape social evils unless he were as blind as a bat, as deaf as a post, or had a heart of stone. National and worldwide social issues ring his doorbell every day and look at him with wistful eyes in every sickroom he visits.

How do Christian ministers plan to play fair with boys who have been three or four years out of high school and never yet had paying jobs? Many such boys are growing shifty and resentful. Through them one visualizes a great group of drifting young men, some of whom are soon to be branded as criminals. They indict our institutions and none more rightly than the church. One remembers that the average age of arrest for 721,000 misdemeanors in New York State in 1930 was under 21 years of age. How many more are there now? How much lower is the average age? What is Christian thinking to say in regard to them? What is Christian social action to do in regard to them? Can the Christian minister evade such a problem? Certainly he cannot. Every honest minister is compelled to search for the Christian solutions of social problems and to work out his ministry upon such answers as he can get from his personal contacts, his studies, his thinking, and any private access he may have to the wisdom of the Almighty.

It is more and more evident that present facts are compelling us all to reshape our thinking about American homes, schools, industrial conditions, unemployment, and the use of leisure time. They require us to bring ourselves up to date in a more courageous ministry than ever before. How can a minister work out his own social philosophy and message soundly unless he think through his own first-hand experiences with people till he sees the far-flung social issues involved in them? How else will he avoid on the one hand a narrow, conservative parochialism, or on the other hand a doctrinaire social radicalism? His own experiences may indeed make him more radical than any mere theory could ever do, but if so it will be as a Christian and on the basis of realized facts.[2]

His prayer will be:

> Open my eyes to visions girt
> With beauty, and with wonder lit—
> But let me always see the dirt,
> And all that spawn and die in it.

[2] Since the question may be raised, it had better be answered in advance. The author is not only not a Communist; he is a disbeliever in Communism, lock, stock and barrel (its gun not his). He isn't even a Socialist. He isn't even a Democrat. He has been a registered Republican for forty years and intends to remain so, exercising his rights of independent judgment within his party as a free American citizen. (Where, pray tell, is an independent more greatly needed?) He has never espoused any social philosophy whatsoever save a thoroughgoing democracy and a vital Christianity.

A PERSON-MINDED MINISTRY

Open my ears to music; let
   Me thrill with Spring's first flutes and drums—
But never let me dare forget
   The bitter ballads of the slums.

From compromise and things half-done,
   Keep me, with stern and stubborn pride;
But when, at last, the fight is won,
   God, keep me still unsatisfied.[3]

Persons have human rights. This second reason for a minister's social concern is especially an American reason. It is based on our whole history of belief in basic human rights. American citizens have fundamental rights as persons, including the right to stand on those rights and to exercise them as free men in a free society. When those rights are in jeopardy in any area of American life then Christians, especially ministers, have a duty as straight as a pikestaff.

The plain facts are that even in America society as it now is breaks in upon and breaks up persons, pollutes them, frustrates them, thwarts them, and degrades them in suffering that is socially originated and is ever with us. There are vast masses of such persons. Only recently the President of this richest nation on earth confessed publicly that at least one-third of our people are undernourished, underclothed, and inadequately housed, with unknown millions unemployed. That states it only on the most elementary physical level. It says nothing of the heartache and heartbreak, the illness of mind and spirit in great sections of our American people. But persons must not be violated, in America of all places. They must be validated as persons. We must keep at least one spot on earth as decent as we can. Well might Bishop Francis J. McConnell say in the Cornell University chapel, "It is

---

[3] Louis Untermeyer, "Prayer." From *Selected Poems and Parodies of Louis Untermeyer*. By permission of Harcourt, Brace & Co.

blasphemous that men should go hungry in the very midst of plenty. There is something profane and irreverent about that." He had evidently been meditating upon the sacredness of persons and the fact that human beings have rights in their own humanity. As human beings they have inalienable rights to "life, liberty, and the pursuit of happiness." For this our exiled fathers crossed the sea, and thousands upon thousands of other people wish they could do so today. Nothing short of a clean demonstration of validated human rights and a world outreach of unselfishness is demanded of America today!

Jesus dreamed a realistic dream. The Christian minister has this third reason for social concern. Long ago in Palestine a Young Man dreamed a dream. He took an old political nationalistic hope of His people and re-dreamed it in a vision called a "Kingdom"—both a spiritual order within people and a new society of people in which justice, righteousness, and love should be socially established. That Kingdom is not and will not be achieved until persons of every sort—all persons— shall be validated as persons. Even such validation is only the beginning of what it would mean for men and women to be wholly redeemed and given full opportunity to become grown-up sons and daughters of the Eternal. In that Kingdom the whole of life for all people is sacred, and they are to live abundantly therein with radiant happiness; that, to Him, is the meaning of the Kingdom.

Is this a dead conception buried in Palestine long ago? It seems to be so in the minds of some ministers; the word "Kingdom" a sort of other-world word, a kind of thin pale word in the unrealistic phraseology which afflicts so much the vocabulary of many ministers. Can the Kingdom be sidetracked into some psychological dead-end of ministerial phraseology? No, not with the world-transforming power there is in Jesus and His dream. *Today* He says, "I appoint unto you a Kingdom." In that Kingdom there shall be no Brahmin nor untouchable low-caste men, no patrician nor plebian, no royalty nor commoner. "The only royalty is nobility."

We come, therefore, to the minister's part in the achievement of the new social order in New York and Pennsylvania, in Louisiana, California, Arkansas, and all other states of the Union. It is a realistic job with real persons as they are and as they may become in all our cities, villages, and rural areas. The minister is to be co-creator of an order of society in America in which persons shall be both truly validated and wholly redeemed. This might be called the prophetic ministry were it not the habit of so many so-called prophets to take it all out in talk. But the creation of a new social order out of present-day conditions takes more than talk. One need not go farther than the congested areas of any great American city, the historic section of New Orleans, for example, with its combination of underworld and slum, nor farther than the pitiful negro cabins along the shores of Mississippi bayous to find what we mean. A girl in those slums, a boy in those swamps—what chance have they for valid growth in normal life as Jesus conceived it? What chance have they in the bedraggled camps of migrant laborers or in the back tenement alleys of Baltimore or Washington? There are spots of subnormal living in every one of our great cities and rural sections, north, south, east, and west. In our industries and economic processes there are forces of social and racial injustice that take their heaviest toll from the weakest, the most ignorant, the most defenseless persons among us. Why should American ministers see Jesus less vividly in such American sag-spots than Francis Thompson saw Him in the London slums:

> Not where the wheeling systems darken,
> And our benumbed conceiving soars!—
> The drift of pinions, would we harken,
> Beats at our own clay-shuttered doors.

The angels keep their ancient places;—
   Turn but a stone, and start a wing!
'Tis ye, 'tis your estranged faces,
   That miss the many-splendoured thing.

But (when so sad thou canst not sadder)
   Cry;—and upon thy so sore loss
Shall shine the traffic of Jacob's ladder
   Pitched betwixt Heaven and Charing Cross.

Yea, in the night, my Soul, my daughter,
   Cry,—clinging Heaven by the hems;
And lo, Christ walking on the water
   Not of Genesareth, but Thames! [4]

CHRISTIAN SOCIAL ACTION BY OUR FOUR ESSENTIALS OF METHOD

By what methods shall a Christian minister seek to establish the realm of love in America? Here come into play the same essentials of method we have earlier stressed.

By achieving togetherness. The first essential for a minister is to do everything in his power to establish a sense of togetherness with all possible persons, especially with all who call themselves Christians—honest men among employers, owners, and landlords who acknowledge social obligations as well as rights and seek to fulfill these obligations as Christians. He should likewise establish a sense of togetherness with all employed persons, laborers, and tenants who acknowledge their obligations as well as rights and who also seek as Christians to fulfill their obligations however difficult. It is essential to magnify mutuality of interest and concern between rich and poor, colored and white, dwellers in city and country, producers and consumers, merchants and customers. This is indispensable if spiritual unity "one and indivisible," as well

[4] Francis Thompson, "In No Strange Land." By permission of Dodd, Mead & Co.

as liberty, is ever to be achieved in the Republic, if America is to do her duty toward a world realm of Universal Love.

The specific methods of social action cannot and must not be prescribed by any one person nor by any oligarchy. Honest and courageous experimentation in the arts of conciliation and joint effort will gradually set us onward toward the goal. The solution will be no single political movement, social crusade, administrative action, nor legislative enactment. Such of these as are tested by time and found not wanting will be fused with other factors into a multiple solution. But they must be achieved by free men in a free society. A basic determination to get as many men of good will as possible to work together in this warfare for social justice and the common good is the first essential. What a ministry of reconciliation awaits all ministers ordained and unordained!

By relentless pursuit of social facts. The second method is the getting and facing of the facts that make a difference with human well-being. Since when have Christians acquired any right to be socially ignorant or lethargic persons? Who gave them any such liberty? Who gave any minister a right to brand devoted social scientists or other scientists as anti-Christian because in their pursuit of the truth they turn up some new facts which do not fit in with some old ideas? What are the actual facts? This is the one point that matters. What is true? Christian ministers, of all persons, have everything to gain from the truth, nothing to fear, nothing to lose.

No single man or school of searchers can either set or limit with finality the specific methods of social inquiry. Scientific social inquiry itself is a developing process, free upward free truthward. Fact-getting has to be as free from slavish traditionalism and dogmatic limitation of method as the free flowing of a mighty river. Its currents find their own levels. Unseen laws control them in their passage toward the ocean of truth they seek. No one person nor any group of persons can shut off any area of human experience from the free play of the truth-seeking spirit of man. The unvarnished truth about American social conditions is the indispensable basis for intelligent social action. Patiently and tirelessly to get and make sure of the facts about situations and conditions as well as persons—is a minister's indubitable obligation. What minister wants to use any other method than the open method of honest search for truth? The tension between our social facts and the vision of Jesus will continue to spur us on.

By deeper realization of the meanings of social facts. This leads us, thirdly, to consider ways and means by which the realization of the meaning of ascertained social facts and the acceptance of such facts as facts shall be achieved by the largest numbers of persons. Social fact-facing and realization were never more needed in America than today. Each person must discover his own best means of realization, whether in first-hand observation and effort, in well chosen reading, in meditation and prayer, in conference, or in all of these. True realization calls for all the means to social-spiritual understanding in the inmost souls of men and women. The very inadequacy of some of us ministers as "realizers" of social evils may be a prime source of difficulty in the achievement of constructive social change. Most of us need to be forced out more often from our own parishes into sag-spots of poverty and mass suffering if we are ever to realize deeply "how the other half lives." We might thus come to a more realistic awareness that we are on trial as to our leadership in creating a realm of love out of present-day society. Our own larger ministry to all those in need, more intercessory prayer for them, deeper commitment to the purposes of Jesus might then ensue. The hunger of people for divine response through us might bring us afresh to the Answerer of human need. The means of realization in us and in our people would thus be deepened. Those who sense, even a little, the volume of human tragedy and the reality of divine response find themselves prepared profoundly to work with social passion for the achievement of the realm of love.

By considered action. Finally, in the fourth place, better methods of social action must come into their own in all areas of social need. Violent and hasty action, emotional and selfish action will be seen as destructive of creative relationships rather than as aids to truth and justice. Inaction, on the other hand, is equally indefensible. A sole devotion to the ultimate ends of universal social justice by means of love will be seen as the desperate need it is in human affairs. Freedom of honest experimentation in methods will be seen as essential for this supremely difficult achievement. The basic rights of freedom of speech, freedom of worship, and the right of assembly must at the very least be maintained. When civil liberties are filched away in any area or industry, there the very foundations of social justice are undermined. In a democratic society the the methods of social action must be kept free from suppression and autocratic control. True methods arise out of the creative experience of living persons as they wrestle with the forces of evil in the common life. When ministers, ordained and unordained, espouse the arts of social reconstruction by means of well-considered action, their methods refine themselves as they move toward the great goal of universal well-being in the spirit of Him who is their Leader and Perfecter of their faith, their action, and their love. They will not forget His courage as he drove the money changers from the temple, challenged the scribes and Pharisees as hypocrites, and befriended those in need.

Who if not the Christian groups in America are obligated to lead the fight against war, to democratize industry and help break unemployment, to establish adequate relief for the poor while working for the ultimate elimination of poverty, to break the stranglehold of special interest groups, to

198

fight for freedom of speech, to eliminate race prejudice, to socialize selfishly accumulated wealth, to replace the profit motive with the motive of sharing, to vitalize education, to release women to full partnership with men, to give all boys and girls a fair chance at the good things of life, to universalize mental hygiene on Christian levels, and to fight for all the concrete social values which are essential to the new social order? For freedom did Christ set men free, yet not till all Christians and most of all His ministers learn how to suffer more deeply with all beleaguered persons shall the Kingdom come.

ALL CHRISTIANS MAY AID IN ACHIEVING THE REALM OF LOVE

Every Christian in the priesthood of all believers must be free to choose from the wide array of social methods and causes now being espoused by earnest men and women those which in good conscience under the highest leadership he can devotedly pursue. In the far distant future by multiple constructive efforts shall the universal realm of love be realized in human life. Then and then only shall there be a social order in which it will be safe for the lamb and the lion to lie down together and for a little child to lead them.

> The world's old;
> But the old world waits the hour to be renewed,
> Toward which new hearts in individual growth
> Must quicken, and increase to multitude
> In new dynasties of the race of men,
> Developed whence shall grow spontaneously
> New churches, new economies, new laws
> Admitting freedom, new societies
> Excluding falsehood: He shall make all new.[5]

He? Yes, but not without us! He—we, shall make all new.

[5] Elizabeth Barrett Browning, "Aurora Leigh."

IX

THE MINISTER AS INTERPRETER OF ETERNAL PERSONAL VALUES

MODERNS ARE ABSORBED BY THINGS OF LITTLE VALUE

HIGH-POWERED salesmanship has done a thorough job in the psychology of America. It has aimed at the people's attention and got it. They are now well "sold." Gadgets by the millions have been sold to persons by the million—good gadgets no doubt, comfortable and convenient ones. But what about the persons who have been sold to the gadgets? They are the point—persons sold to a gadgety life. Many a momentarily prosperous young urbanized couple lives that kind of a life, only that and nothing more—nothing except the installments yet to be paid on the gadgets. Professor E. A. Ross once said, "The modern gadgets are wonderful triumphs of engineering ingenuity, but when the day comes that we have a foolproof device for doing everything we have to do we will have a world fit only for fools to live in." The necessity of mastering difficulties gives qualities to persons which gadgets cannot give, but which they can take away. There is native resource power in the men of the mountains, forests, farms, and ships that many an urbanized man has lost. No softies they!

Supersalesmen! Go right on "selling" us and softening our life by introducing your wares with your arted oily voices over the radio and over the telephone, and with your blaring signs in sylvan nooks, till no unsullied spot is left, not even the bedroom nor the sky. Go right on insidiously encouraging us into debt by nicely graduated installment plans—interest at only fourteen per cent on unpaid balances. Help us to become heedless of our unpaid bills, unbothered by bankruptcy itself. You are succeeding wonderfully; you will soon have us made completely into the kind of persons you want us to be, suggestible, gullible persons, or bitter because we realize at last that we have been "sold" to the loudest loud speaker. That is, you will if we let you and fail to realize that sales resistance is one of the realest of all virtues under the present system. But it isn't the goods that matter, for some of them are a human benefit and a delight. It isn't even debts of themselves that matter crucially. It is the people themselves who matter, for they are priceless. Their deeper cravings, their unpostponable deeper needs also cry for attention and get it not, because you have stolen away their basic spiritual experiences with it. Attention is essential, as essential as impregnation if there is ever to be a birth of anything priceless like a great idea, a great poem, or a child. You know better than most of us that people become like the things to which they attend, thingy-minded if they pay attention only to gadgets and other things.

Enduring values are the distillates, the winnowings of basic human experience. If that experience is a softy's experience, the values will be pasty values because the men will be papier-maché men—mere boudoir men, highly perfumed and sleek.

How strange that old Isaiah had to have it out about the same sort of stuff that got into Israel from effeminate Egypt, or elsewhere round about, centuries ago. He described people of a certain stripe as those "that weave a web but not of my spirit," saith the Lord, "that say to the seers, See not; and to the prophets, Prophesy not unto us right things, speak unto us smooth things, prophesy deceits." (Urban lady readers, if any, will take delight in Isaiah 3:16-4:6, and in the whole of Isaiah 32. Moulton's *Modern Reader's Bible* is suggested.) In every age, ancient or modern, values are the winnowings of experience. The vigor and the rightness of the experience determines the intrinsic worth of the values, the cleanness of the wheat.

St. Paul puts it this way:

Whatsoever things are true, whatsoever things are honorable, whatsoever things are just, whatsoever things are pure, whatsoever things are lovely, whatsoever things are of good report; if there be any virtue, and if there be any praise, think on these things.[1]

These are all the qualities of persons, qualities possessed by persons, qualities illuminated by persons—the bubbling playfulness of little children; the native cleanness of boys and girls; all that is radiant in young womanhood; all that is steady and able in men and women to bear adversity; all that is beautiful beyond words in motherhood; the heroic that emerges in common men when flood, fire, pestilence, or the horror of war stalk in our midst; all in men of social vision that aspires and endures and gives itself with abandon to great causes; all in the aged that is resourceful and wise.

These all are qualities of persons, high personal values, distilled out of basic human experience. These give life its meanings.

> Fool! all that is, at all,
> Lasts ever, past recall; . . . .
> What entered into thee,
> That was, is, and shall be. . . . .[2]

IN ORDER TO DISCOVER THE MINISTER MUST ADVENTURE INTO THE BEYOND

Discovering is an essential process. Before he interprets a minister must discover. Else he will have nothing to interpret. He has to discover values for himself—great, basic, enduring

[1] Philippians 4:8.
[2] Robert Browning, "Rabbi Ben Ezra."

values that other men are searching for and want him to help them find. When will he ever learn that he cannot use as his own other people's findings and make them authentic? They must be his own, authentically his own, winnowed free from chaff, the clean sound wheat of his own experience. That sort of wheat is seminal. It germinates. Failure at this point means spiritual sterility for ministers and for the churches no fields white unto harvest.

First there is the danger for ministers who are often tempted by fatigue, by overloads of work, by futile distractions, to use as their own materials that are not their own. They often keep on hand collections of other men's sermons upon which they draw liberally. Furthermore, they are besieged by mail-order salesmen to buy "model sermons, one just right for every occasion, beautifully illustrated, true to life, ethical quality guaranteed. Double choices are provided for every Sabbath in the year. They help you to 'get by' on a heavy Sunday after a busy week. Two dollars the set, mailed in a sealed envelope without label. Buy these 'original' sermons now and have them ready in reserve." To take and to use another person's product without giving credit to the author—that is to plagiarize. That is the sin of sins among literary folk who have coined themselves into their product, but it is not yet so acknowledged among all ministers. The parallel trick in other areas is plain stealing, a crime called "theft."

There are subtle dangers for the churches also, both local churches and denominations, for they, as well as their ministers, must have and share authentic Christian experience if they are truly to interpret insights that are born of the spirit of God. One notes, for example, in certain village churches the increasing use of copyrighted materials, prayers and paragraphs more or less prescribed for use in worship services. They are evidently fabricated in some general staff headquarters, sometimes well prepared and in better form than the local minister might do them. The intent is obvious, to heighten the felicity of the worship service, to give local point to the national wave of interest in an embellished ritual. But we ask, what is a ritual? Never an end in itself. Rather a means to an end. If it includes an historic prayer that has repeatedly borne aloft a weight of human aspiration, is refined in its wording, is pregnant with spiritual meanings, and is to be shared as in a fellowship of age-old yearning, then such a prayer is truly a means to an.end. Replete with human experience it catches the worshipers up and out to the universal and the eternal. But even with such a prayer one would not close one's eyes to the dangers in the habitual use of anything that may become a prescribed form of words, a convenient crutch to lean upon if only the intonations be made to sound authentic though the mind be far away. A deeper danger is present for the minister not trained to worthy uses of ritual, trained rather, if at all, to follow the impulse of the moment. Some, indeed, are accustomed to open the mouth without any previous preparation, in hope that the Lord will fill it. But now there comes to this local church neither majestic ancient prayer nor message of renewed confidence in the inner light. Instead come these improvised materials intended to convey denominational ideals and generalized aspirations which ought to be "all right" almost anywhere. They are prepared for the "special" Sundays now so frequent. On regular Sundays the local minister can do well enough by himself, but for the high holy days helps must be sent. Is he inspired by them to fresh discoveries of his own so that he may say what ought to be said better than he has ever said it before? If so, splendid! And that is exactly what some of the most helpful aids to worship supply, with suggestions of several possible choices and with open spaces for original elements. But if general staff headquarters say it all for the minister and prescribe it to him—no. Some great churches, neither trusting nor quickening the inner light, nor giving their ministers either prayer books or beads, muddy their own spiritual waters. Why not trust the inner light or else move frankly to the explicit regimentation of spiritual experiences in seemly order on ecclesiastical schedule like the convinced ritualists? Or else why not speak in an unknown tongue like the Roman Catholics, whose principle of procedure, like it or not, is as clear as a bell?

Why do we not wholeheartedly trust and nourish the inner light? Aided by suggestions, if he needs them, every person-minded minister might freshly discover for himself and in the living experiences of his people the realities that then and there need emphasis. He might wrestle with the Eternal for his own message and for the putting of it. Why should he not battle for it as Paul, Cephas, and Apollos? Any minister and any people who cease to discover spiritual values for themselves in their own experience will lack the vivid sense of reality needed for creative relations' s.

There are kindred issues which involve individual initiative, democratic procedure, and the discovery of values on the part of all Christians through freedom to do independent thinking and creative work. For example, will the new Methodism, largest of Protestant church groups with its twenty-five thousand ministers and eight million members, pray more earnestly than ever before for quickened spiritual insights on the part of all its ministers and its people; for fresh discoveries of the nature of man, the Grace of God, and His Salvation, so that free men may become sons of God (sic John Wesley)? Or shall the new Methodism follow the methods of instructional regimentation familiar to American big business? Shall her bishops and boards hand down orders to local ministers as if to retail salesmen at the end of a chain-store line? Might one respectfully suggest to the Methodist bishops (or any other group of ecclesiastical executives, Lords Temporal or Spiritual) that at their next conclave, after the first devotional service has been opened with prayer, and with scripture from the authorized canon (possibly John 13: 12-17), the following passage from the American canon, written by Saint William James, be read and then repeated in unison: "As for me, my bed is made. I am against bigness and greatness in all their forms and with the invisible molecular forces that work from individual to individual stealing in through the crannies of the world like so many soft rootlets or like the capillary oozing of water, and yet rending the hardest monuments of man's pride if you give them time. The bigger the unit you deal with, the hollower, the more brutal, the more mendacious is the life displayed. So I am against all big organizations as such, national ones first and foremost, against all big successes and big results, and in favor of all the eternal forces of truth which always work in individuals—underdogs always—till history comes after they are long dead and puts them on top."[3] Saints, apostles, prophets, martyrs answer with a loud "amen"; and so do the scientists, the artists, and the poets.

The method necessary for the discovery of spiritual values is no mere maintenance of efficiency in a mammoth organization with multiple parts all fitly joined together, running smoothly, and adding to the plant daily such extensions as should be made. The very plant might in the end take precedence over the product. Many of us non-Methodists watch and pray with a great affection and with some sense of the volume of human destiny involved that spiritual creativity may continue to spring up in Methodist churches by direct light and leading of the Eternal, in little groups of worshiping, witnessing Christians everywhere. It is possible surely for creativity in spiritual relationships to operate in small living groups of free men and women under the highest leadership even in a vast aggregation of such groups, provided they con-

[3] *Letters of William James,* edited by his son Henry James, Little, Brown & Co., Boston, 1920, II, 90.

tinue to be such groups and do not become something quite other. Such groups operate by the same laws and inner lights as those which quicken individual men and women to discover the unsearchable riches of the grace of God in all creative relationships.

What has the minister to interpret? Nothing? Or something in the Beyond? The disbelievers in the "common" man, in the "ordinary" minister say brutally: "The plain fact is they haven't any creativity—nothing of their own to say. They are poverty stricken in the midst of plenty. Each of them should be placarded, 'No News,' and thus described: This early winter morning, in the sunbright mountains, as we stopped at the very station of 'Rising Springs,' a great hulk of a man rushed down the aisle to buy a penny paper, feverish for outside news, for a cocktail of printer's ink—black draught to set his blood aflowing. No news of his own this morning. No news from glittering mountain tops or swaying pines. No news from curving sweeps of freshly fallen snow. No news from mountain waters flashing down with music from the mouth of God. No news of the Everlasting leaping in his arteries. No mighty currents throbbing warm with glowing words. No news for the valleys far below. No news of his own. No news. No news!"

Are the ministers we know insensitive and vacuous like that? Hardly. But suppose we were all to admit that on some Monday mornings we feel like that—no response to outside glory, no flaming light within—flat, plain flat. Sometimes all ministers, along with other artists and social workers, feel like that. But that's fatigue, not inner darkness. It is merely fatigue, to be cured by swapping stories on a carefree hike, by a fishing trip, or a hoe handle and watering pot in the garden, or a horseback ride, or whatever you like.

Yet the brutal disbeliever in ministers retorts, "Some of you

are like that all the time—always flat, always 'No News.'"
Maybe so. (It might be I, and I know it not.) But perhaps
the man he has in memory was some natively timid soul
always easily abashed, much put upon in childhood, and never
since released to autonomous manhood, now escaped into a
sedentary life with a whole panoply of safety-first devices,
housebound, never allowed to go out without his rubbers, never
an adventurous night out (not a single coon hunt), never an
exhilarating battle over anything—not even croquet.

There may be a few who are flat like that—flat with fear
and inanition—but we plead not guilty. Not guilty the ministers who have shared our searches. Not so A.W., with a
mind like a surgeon's scapel; not so witty P.G., who knows
and loves his people family by family in the bottom lands of
Arkansas; not so R.T., who oozes verse and vision; not so
H.C., undaunted rider of an impossible Methodist circuit;
nor E.B., of deep, determined will; nor J.W., as lovable as the
John for whom he was named; nor W.C., of architectural
genius; nor "Brother Jim," obviously of arboreal ancestry;
not so J.H., and wife, a dedicated team, intelligent to their
fingertips; nor E.D., modest soul with an unrealized literary
gift; nor J.S., calm, wise, judicial; nor M.S., brave and brilliant; not so Elder L., long-distance Texas ranger, six feet
four; not so the boys in the School of Theology at S. M. U.,
braving heavy odds in preparing to minister in the wide areas
of windy Texas. Frigid North! Effete East! Look to your
laurels when such men as these are in the lists! And as for
you, cynical disbeliever in ministers, kindly make your way
to the rear and sit down quietly where you belong. Please
don't disturb the meeting again. (Let's see, where were we?
Speaking of flatness. Oh yes.)

There is a flatness we would all own up to, a flatness that
comes from busyness, from over-absorption in the here and
now, that makes us forget the Beyond. We fail to keep aware

of it, daily to make new sallies into it, and so fail to make discoveries within it.

To get up and out of the here and now, out of "the ring of the rueful neighbors," out of the local (both geographical and mental), out to the universal; to go adventuring "beyond the ranges"; to find a clean, bright pool to swim in where we've never swum before, somewhere in the Beyond—that is our need.

There is a Beyond!

Beyond
    All the mechanisms of our life,
    The checkerboards of city streets,
    The journeys and appointments,
    The smooth society of neatly complacent minds,
      —there is a Beyond.

The gateways are not far away.
    "One key is solitude, and silence one."
    The wind in the pines,
    The lights upon the hills,
    The canyon paths, afoot or horseback
    To the haunts of living creatures in the winter woods,
    Wild birds against the sky,
    The river gleaming in the sun,
    The ancient ocean steeped in mystery,
    The night sky and the familiar stars.

Yet closer by
    The circle round the hearth at eventide,
    The eyes that love us,
    Children,
    The Beyond that is within.

While never far away
Are heartache and
The needs of human kind.
These all are gateways to the Great Beyond.

How adventure and where? How shall one learn to discover in the Beyond? By adventuring there. Discovery is no longer stumbling on a pot of gold. Discovery depends upon adventuring, intelligent planned adventuring, like Byrd's to the South Pole, skillfully planned, skillfully executed.

How adventure and where?

Inward. First "the Beyond that is within."

One key is solitude, and silence one.

To adventure within—where a still, small voice is whispering, "Come speak with me in quietness." So someday while the clock ticks in your silent study (as in mine this frosty sunlit morning), listen while the warm sun speaks, time speaks, love speaks, the very walls and memories of an old and sacred home life speak. They say, "You too have a 'little postern gate to God.' Why not use it?" Please to

Be still and listen,
Be still and drink the quiet
Of all round.[4]

Then a voice whispers, "He that hath ears to hear, let him listen. I have many things to say unto you, but you are not yet ready to listen to Me. Even if your ears were to hear the words I have to say to you, you have no deeper receptivities prepared. You wouldn't realize the meaning of them; so I can't even say them. Couldn't you get yourself cleared of all anxiety and all bitterness this morning? There are some Great Words I want to say to you as soon as you are ready"—so

[4] Edward Rowland Sill, "Peace."

> Rest with palms folded;
> Rest with thine eyelids fallen—
> Lo!   Peace is here.[5]

The Beyond that is within—I must adventure often here.

Outward.   Out!   To the out-of-doors I must go—in sunlight or by starlight, deep in the forest or out on the rounded hills, under the whispering hemlocks or by an ocean shore, by some deep lake of peace or down the river canoeing, ostensibly so, but really listening, looking, absorbing bits of the nameless beauty—catching flashes here and there of the light that never was on sea or land.

> O all wide places, far from feverous towns!
> Great shining seas! pine forests! mountains wild!
> Rock bosomed shores! rough heaths! and sheep-cropped downs!
> Vast pallid clouds! blue spaces undefiled!
> Room! give me room! give loneliness and air!
> Free things and plenteous in your regions fair.[6]

The Beyond that is without—I must often go adventuring there.

Downward!   Deep down into human tragedy!   The multiple exploitations of the underworld, vice and crime—these the minister must understand.   Past the hard glitter of its night-life lights, past the tricky lures neatly set for innocents, past the gaily painted fronts of noisome places and noisome persons, straight to the heart of the sin and suffering that are masked there, he must go.   Some errand of mercy may take him—mere curiosity never.   There are women from his region there, possibly from his own town.   No one else respects them. He should reverence them too much to spy upon them. Spirited girls they were, who had "a fuss with Dad," maybe,

---

[5] *Ibid.*

[6] George MacDonald.   From *Poems of George MacDonald,* published by E. P. Dutton & Co., Inc., New York.

and flung away in anger from the village drabness, "just to see a bit of city life." "Something happened." Time wore on. They never came back. Boys from the region are there too, boys who "went to the city." Most of them went straight. Some went broke. Some went wrong and are now "big money makers." Their sources of income are not revealed, especially not to the government. Why do they never write the home folks anymore, nor come back to the village? (Or maybe they do ostentatiously.)

Could a person-minded minister by any chance find a lost boy or girl for an aging mother who sits by her fire alone, crooning a long-forgotten, ridiculed song, "Oh where is my wandering boy tonight, the child of my love and care"? Favorite jest in some circles. Prodigal son, ha! ha! Material for sob-stuff appeals in other circles, but stark reality in the broken circle of too many American homes! Is there no such reality left in the modern world as redeeming love? Has even the sense of it all been ridiculed away? Or did someone leave a trust fund of it, an ample fund? It is reported that any modern person can get access to it by matching his own contribution with it. Ministers are said to be the trustees of that inheritance! Adventurous trustees!

Or is human tragedy to be found in some slum area, unbelievably congested with persons, with no solitude, no quiet, no more privacy than a loincloth would provide, and located often just next door to the night life which is near in more ways than by physical location? Here are acres upon acres of persons, thousands upon thousands of persons, all compactly arranged in tenement tiers, that go high up and deep down. These are areas where poverty and hunger are forced into the same streets and houses with vice and crime, where sodden men and women pollute the innocence of children, where young boys go in gangs whose members efficiently teach one another, where girls early learn to hunt for pleasure in pairs or alone, where the bodies of fresh young women are bought and sold for a price, and where gaiety rarely comes unless it is both faked and blasted with alcohol. Here are the depressed classes of the hungry, cold, and unemployed. Here are the persons who are on relief rolls (maybe). Here are suffering *and* courage, heartache *and* victory (ye gods, what courage and what victories). Here also is congestion *and* loneliness. Here is the home of artificial flowers, here long-drawn defeat and exploited funerals. Does any love surround all this handiwork of man's exploitation? All this tragedy? Unbelievable Love. What an adventure!

Or possibly human tragedy never left the farm or the village. There goes "Old Hank" now, shuffling, staggering up the street, his labor power exploited by well-to-do farmers all his life, lust all burned out long ago, hard-cider-drunk again today —old jailbird out for the "autumn season." Not much *sacré* hovering around "Old Hank" this morning, nothing visible in that weak old faccid face save the vestiges of mercurial spent desires, naught save a glint in the watery eye when I thrust him through with my rapier jibe; but that much is a flash of the lovable, humorous, human being "Old Hank" used to be, not yet quite burned to the socket's rim. (Nobody cares a hang about lousy Old Hank. You don't, you know you don't.) But—

> Did Someone promise a love so great?
> Must he die like that in hell too late?

The Beyond that is downward—I must often go adventuring there.

Backward. If the wholesale bruising and marring of persons ever gets a man's real attention, if he ever deeply senses the blighting and the hurt of human life—what it is that vice, crime, and economic exploitations do to persons—and if he understands the suicidal intensification of these destructive powers by the mania of war, he cries out in anguish for an absolutely honest interpretation of human tragedy. He demands to know where human tragedy comes from, what it is and what it does to persons, what it means for the future of the race. What can be done about it? Who has the answers to it? What are they? His youthful glibness has suddenly departed now. His easy lightness has set in colors of a darker hue, but is all suffused with lambent flame.

> "What's in the scroll," quoth he, "thou keepest furled?
>   Show me their shaping,
> Theirs who most studied man, the bard and sage—
>   Give!" [7]

Humbly he goes into quiet places where the interpreters live and work, study and think, create and sometimes pray. As in spacious rooms not made of clay, the interpreters have been working through the ages—often best in the interludes of public action. He will find there interpretations wise and fantastic, pictures in true perspective and distorted landscapes, music that obscures, music that obsesses, but also great symphonies that lift up the still, sad music of humanity and give it wings of throbbing flight. "Each sufferer says his say, his scheme of the weal and woe."

But he will have nothing now save the absolute best. No longer can the superficial answers content him, nor bizarre pictures, nor tricky music—exhibitionistic things done for mere effect. No interpretations that deny the reality of evil or sin or suffering can ever satisfy him. The truth, the whole truth, nothing but the truth about humanity—its bruising and its healing—can ever satisfy his soul again. And so above all in his adventure he will search out the familiar great interpretations that have borne the weight of human healing:

[7] Robert Browning, "A Grammarian's Funeral."

214

the scriptures well worn by human use, the great hymns, the great prayers and litanies, the "Sistine Madonna," Beethoven's "Sixth Symphony," Shakespeare's great tragedies, "The Winged Victory"—interpretations that portray and find and heal the soul of man, essentially unchanging as it is through the centuries. So to live always "in the presence of the best," the best music, pictures, books, and persons—the finest persons, the humblest, bravest, most spiritually mature—that will result in the qualitation of his life. That will give him, in due season, something to say, much to interpret.

Of all the books, one book he will find that men singularly call *the* Book because it interprets best and answers most their immemorial heartache, their hungers and their hopes. Here is a fresh word about it from a journalist:

Certain of our wise men of today have shaded away sin till it becomes an expression of temperament. They tell us that we sin because our grandfather sinned, and because our home is situated in the wrong block. These are clever words of clever comforters, and surely they ought to wipe away forever the tears from our eyes. But we do not ask that our sin shall be explained. We wish forgiveness and a fresh start. In the Book we no longer read, there are no soft words about sin. But the way out is shown. And here, too, is comfort in plenty for man broken by his toil and his grief.

When again will any company of writers say the things they know in such telling words—the boy far from the faces of his home and far gone in shame? Much is swept away between us and them, but not one accent of Naomi's voice is lost to us, and still the "Turn again, my daughter," is as wistful as when it breathed through the alien corn.

What richer consolation are we hungry for that we turn from Judea?

Is our science so acute that it has banished failure from man's life?

Have our ships sailed so far that they have revealed to us a braver continent than the fields where pain once reigned?

Has the human heart changed under the wear of the centuries, so that sin no longer seeks forgiveness, and grief has no need of a comforter? [8]

The Beyond that is backward—I must often go adventuring there.

Upward. Having seen and sensed something of the meaning of all this, the minister is ready now to fare forth with his own interpretation, sure of great things he would say, enduring values he would communicate. But a gentle hand is laid on his shoulder and a quiet voice inquires, "Were you going alone? Did you think you were ready? Hadn't you better take Someone with you? It seems always to be best that way."

Years ago in the old Dwight Hall at Yale, George Adam Smith, great Scot, great adventurer, and great interpreter of the Bible, made some of us see a thing about adventuring, never seen before, but ever remembered since. He had been up and away on a mountain climb in Switzerland, he told us,

---

[8] Arthur Gleason, *Love, Home and the Inner Life,* F. A. Stokes & Co., New York. This word is from the pen of a man who risked his life, a ransom for many, for the many wounded men whom he rescued as a stretcher bearer from the hell spots of Belgian cities in the First World War. Imperishable Arthur! His quality of life was like the freshness of morning and the calm of evening. Philip Gibbs wrote to the *London Chronicle* of him after the Germans shelled Dixmude to pieces October 21, 1914: "Among the stretcher bearers was an American journalist named Gleason, who had put aside his pen for a while to do manual work in fields of agony, proving himself to be a man of calm quiet courage, always ready to take great risks in order to bring in a stricken soldier. I did not guess that we had been asked to go into the open mouth of death. . . . . I was in one of the ambulances and Gleason sat behind me between the stretchers. Over my shoulder he talked in a quiet voice of the job that lay before us. I was glad of that quiet voice, so placid in its courage. A mass of masonry crashed down from the portico. Some still dark forms lay among the fallen stones. There was never a moment when shell-fire was not bursting in that square about us. The shrapnel bullets whipped the stones. Gleason was already taking down a stretcher. He had a little smile about his lips. I caught sight of a heap of huddled bodies. What others were doing I don't know, except that Gleason's calm face made a clear-cut image on my brain."

on the Weisshorn, which is more than fourteen thousand feet high. Of it he said,

Most of the way from the hut, which is about half way up to the summit, my guides and I had to cut steps in the ice, and we had taken by turns the duty of cutting the steps; and it had cost us all the time from two in the morning, when we started from the hut, until nine, when we got to the summit. The summit, as the summit generally is in these Swiss Alps, was of boulders and pinnacles of granite fifteen or twenty feet high, too high for snow to rest upon them. When we got to the foot of them, one of the guides who was leading at the time stood aside to let me get first to the top. I sprang up without thinking, and exhilarated by the air and eager to see the view, for it was a splendid morning, I forgot the gale which was blowing from the other side, and exhilarated as I was, I stood up to my full height. I felt myself pulled by the jacket. "Down, Sir! Down on your knees! You are not safe there except on your knees!" [9]

So, and only so, is any adventurer safe—most of all any person who would dare to interpret the deepest meanings of the Christian answers to human need. Prayer keeps him humble in the face of that need, lifts him out of discouragement about it, freshens his resources, calms his fretfulness, sweetens his bitterness, refines his qualities, lifts up his hopes, and challenges him to do his duty in the name of the Eternal as long as his life shall last. All this is so because it brings him afresh to love and to deeper realizations through love of the Eternal Answerer confronting human needs.

THE ADVENTURER DISCOVERS LOVE THE FINAL VALUE

The human yearning for embodied love brings him to Jesus. At long last we learn that

[9] "Prayer," in *Sunday Evening Talks to Yale Undergraduates,* edited by H. B. Wright, New Haven, 1899.

A PERSON-MINDED MINISTRY

When all's done, all tried, all counted here,
All great arts, and all good philosophies,
This love just puts its hand out in a dream,
And straight outreaches all things.[10]

There is understandable hunger in the souls of men for personal answers to their needs. It is understandable because they once were children and psychologically and spiritually still are so. Abstractions chill them. Rightly or wrongly, childishly or with deeper insights than the abstractionists yet understand, they cry out in their need like children crying in the night for some great and tender person. Love as a philosophic concept is one thing, but love in a person is another. A whole person who is love is something yet more. Love in a person is what man, by the very nature of his life history and most meaningful experience, *has* to want. The finer and deeper the experience, the more inevitably so—the dark frustrations of life to the contrary notwithstanding—even more because of them. Those who have suffered longest in the deepest valleys crave an Eternal Person who lives serene upon the tops of the mountains. The Psalmist understood all this and voiced it matchlessly, bringing surcease from fear to endless human beings since he wrote these words:

He that dwelleth in the secret place of the Most High,
Shall abide under the shadow of the Almighty.
I will say of Jehovah, He is my refuge and my fortress;
My God, in whom I trust.[11]

Psalms 48, 90, 121, and 125 might well be read with psychological eyes wide open. All down the ages men have said, "Our souls are restless till they rest in Thee"—*Thee,* not it.

To this deep age-old hunger of the human heart, psycho-

[10] Elizabeth Barrett Browning, "Aurora Leigh."
[11] Psalm 91:1, 2.

logically prepared, experientially prepared for Him, came Jesus. Let these words interpret Him:

To his lovely spirit we bring our sadness and our frailty. His gentle thought knows no alien races, no outcast men nor women. He gathers us all, Jew and Gentile, toil-worn and disinherited, within the healing of his love. We need his homely ways, who had no scorn for unsuccess. We need his simple speech, whose words could touch the heart of grief. He told us whither we go. He told us that we go to a place like a father's house, a place with room enough for all. Many years ago, with a tender ministration, he took away the hurt from troubled hearts, and still the thought of him brings comfort for what is bruised with striving and comradeship for what has never been at home in life. The journey is sweeter with him in company. His care for us is more understanding than the heart of all other friends, for in the hour of need they are sometimes very far away. His love is so sure that we take it for granted, so forgiving that we are careless of it, trusting it as we trust the sun continuing in the heavens. It sends out its gentle rays into the immense emptiness of life. It would wait, sorrowful and full of remembrance, through a lifetime of years. Inside its golden circumference it includes all the wide areas of the human spirit, rising through the radiance of youth to manhood's term of power, and falling away to the final dissolution.[12]

Jesus is the means to the great end. Jesus seems not to have thought of Himself as an end, rather as the means to an end, and that end in persons—in men and women and children who throughout all time in every place should know and understand eternal love in a person. God is a Mysterious and Multiple Person, yet an Understandable Answering Person, a Wonderful Counselor, Quickener of Inner Light and Healing, Source and Ground of all Rightness, Home of all Beautiful Relationships, Builder of a Blessed Communion, Creator of a

[12] Arthur Gleason, "The Galilean," in *Love, Home and the Inner Life,* F. A. Stokes & Co., New York.

New Society, Eternal Assurance and Assurer that right shall triumph over wrong, Everlasting Love.

Once did Eternal and Universal Love break through the veil, embodied in a Person. First-born among many brethren, He and the Father are one, one in perfect quality, understandable perfection, imitable perfection; "Ye therefore shall be perfect as your Heavenly Father is perfect"—the perfection of undying universal love. The length and breadth and depth and height of that love is all ye know of Him, and all ye need to know.

> O Saul, it shall be
> A Face like my face that receives thee; a Man like to me,
> Thou shalt love and be loved by, forever: a Hand like this hand
> Shall throw open the gates of new life to thee! See the Christ stand! [13]

> The very God! think, Abib; dost thou think?
> So, the All-Great, were the All-Loving too—
> So, through the thunder comes a human voice
> Saying, "O heart I made, a heart beats here!
> Face, my hands fashioned, see it in myself!
> Thou hast no power nor mayst conceive of mine,
> But love I gave thee, with myself to love,
> And thou must love me who have died for thee!" [14]

> What if even God
> Were chiefly God by living out Himself
> To an individualism of the infinite,
> Eterne, intense, profuse—still throwing up
> The golden spray of multitudinous worlds
> In measure to the proclive weight and rush
> Of His inner nature, the spontaneous love
> Still proof and outflow of spontaneous life? [15]

[13] Robert Browning, "Saul."
[14] Robert Browning, "An Epistle."
[15] Elizabeth Barrett Browning, "Aurora Leigh."

MINISTER AS INTERPRETER OF ETERNAL VALUES

Adventuring upward one discovers at long last (dare we say it?) the very heart of the Eternal Person. One finds glimpses of Him also now in many very human persons who, confessing it or not, have seen Jesus deeply. They have heard what He said and seen what He did, who He was, how He lived, how He died. In lives of quiet beauty and calm power, they discover in Him and through Him the answers to their deep needs and high desires. As in a slowly developing relationship with some great person—some rarely beautiful person—one is allowed little by little to come into intimacy and to draw aside veil after veil till at last one stands in the holy place within a dedicated life, so in mysterious upreaching for a great companionship men find union with the Eternal Person, and the response of the Eternal brings surcease from pain, forgiveness for sin, release from all captivities, and power to live on radiantly into the unknown future.

THE MINISTER AS AN INTERPRETER

Interpretation is more than translation. At an International Student Service Congress in France in 1934, we heard a young translator, after listening for as much as two or three minutes to a speech in French or English or German, speak back in the two other languages that which had been spoken in the first. He did it without the flicker of an eyelash or a sign of a written note, and went on doing it for hours. That is translation, a process in which the transmitted material is uncolored by the translator. That is not interpretation. The interpreter colors the material with the colors of his own personality, and rightly so.

In efforts to interpret one discovers how to interpret. The surest way for any person to become an interpreter is to begin to interpret and to keep on interpreting. He learns as he does it. It is one of the arts, a great art, slowly and gradually achieved at best. Out of his own soul, by ways that are his very own, like Paul and Cephas, Apollos, and all the rest, he discovers how to give to the world his own gospel, his own individual message. The minister is to be an interpreter of the finest values he has discovered in all his spiritual adventuring. He must, if he be a free man, interpret his own glad tidings in whatever ways he can do it best, so that persons whom he touches shall be quickened, guided, and released into abundant living of their own.

Many great arts of interpretation have brought their gifts to the altar. Many and beautiful arts have been employed to carry the word about Jesus, to transmit and create afresh the meanings that spring from the dynamic, intercreative experiences which emanate from fellowship with Him. The continuance of the experience is of greater importance than the means of its continuance, but the methods attempted are of crucial significance, for if they are unfit methods, they misfit the message and cramp its effective flow. If they are worthy methods and real to the user, they give that flow a breadth and depth that carries great resources to the parched fields of human need with no self-sullying of the waters by the boatman, or if the journey be overland, without a constant jabbing at the oxen or creaking of the cart. Every artist is in duty bound by his own ethical integrity to find not only his own subjects, his own pigments, and his own brushes, but to pursue their use, if need be, through poverty and obscurity. The discipline of the years and apparent failure may give him, as it has to many an artist—like Millet, to cite but one—both the enduring message and the indescribable touch of the brush upon the canvas which combine to create interpretations like "The Angelus," "The Sower," and "The Gleaners."

Painting, sculpture, and mosaic art have contributed their priceless madonnas, their innumerable holy families, saints, martyrs, and heroes of the faith—enshrined on canvas, in stained glass, and in the mosaics of great cathedrals. Interpretation may be likewise by the music of great organs, by choral song, by solo voice, by litany or antiphony. Most of all, perhaps, in music do great hymns interpret spiritual values— "Immortal Love, forever full, forever flowing free"; "Break Thou the bread of life, dear Lord, to me"; "Love divine, all loves excelling, joy of heaven to earth come down"; and many another. Or interpretation may be through drama, long the chief vehicle for communicating religious values, in dialogue, cantata, shadow plays, comedy or tragedy, miracle or morality plays, pageant, pantomime, or motion picture. It may likewise be by literary creation, story-telling, folk tale, creative fiction, essay, or poem, or in reading great literature aloud. It may be also by skilled leading of discussion groups and forums which stimulate persons to the exploration of basic life experiences. Or it may be by leading games and hikes, by simple happy talk with boys and girls. Interpretations are by some best made in the relief of economic distress or by other methods of social work. Some incarnate mutuality by settling down to live in a settlement in the midst of the tragic needs of people in a congested city area; others personify world solidarity in a foreign land. Methods to be chosen will include personal counseling in private, teaching, and administration of religious enterprises. Even a little judicious public speaking might, upon occasion, not be out of place!

But any man's methods of witnessing to the unsearchable riches of the Grace of God must be his own choice—not stereotyped methods superimposed upon him. Unless he discover his own method by experiment and adventure, he will never be a free man freely and fully witnessing for the Jesus of his own experience.

How strange that American Protestantism should have chosen out of all these lovely arts of spiritual communication the one art of preaching as paramount, and made it into the apparently indispensable function, though not the only stereotype. By what manner of interpretation have the two Hebrew and the eleven Greek words used in Scripture to describe different shades of meaning for the processes of spiritual communication been allowed to become contracted to preaching, which is defined as follows: "to proclaim by public discourse, to utter in a sermon, or a formal religious harangue." In the popular mind preaching is identified with hortatory public address to a congregation or audience. Let us be entirely clear in this matter. Our objection is not to preaching, far from it—even hortatory preaching when occasion demands it. The objection is to the disproportionate emphasis upon this one method of communicating spiritual values. For example, the president of a leading theological seminary in writing to expectant churches about candidates he had to offer them mentions only this one qualification as follows: "We have a number of admirable students who can be guaranteed to fill pulpits acceptably if we can procure positions for them." To be an interpreter of Jesus *is* to preach with all the direct power of forthright public speech the unsearchable riches of the Grace of God, but the full interpretation of Jesus is far more than that. The other arts of spiritual communication await a far wider use in American Protestant churches.

Here is an interpretation of the modern ministry. The author would be honest with his thesis and give here an interpretation of his own, spoken out of deep affection to a younger man about to begin his ministry.

After many years of friendship we have come up together, Al, to this most meaningful hour. This is one of the happy moments of life. We give you a fourfold welcome to the Christian ministry.

We welcome you first to hatred and to combat. No man who watches and understands the ramifications of evil in our modern life can fail to agree with Henrik Ibsen that sometimes "the true, the sovereign love is hate." We welcome you to deep hatred of social injustice in modern life, hatred of lust and greed and savage power. First and foremost to hatred of the exploitation of women and girls by the lusts of men, hatred of all agencies of vice and its underworld; to hatred, second, of greed, the exploitation of men and women and children in brutalizing systems of labor and enforced idleness for the sake of selfish private gain; to hatred, third, of savage power which subordinates human values to private profits whenever and wherever it is free to spread itself.

We welcome you to hatred of all systems and agencies of lust and greed and power which bleed the bodies and minds of men and women and children and toss them aside upon the scrap-heaps of society, frustrated, broken, and defeated. We welcome you next to hatred of class and racial scorn which poisons the spirit of our common life, the scorn with which the so-called "higher" classes lord it over the so-called "lower" classes, with which so-called "white folks" lord it over so-called "black folks." We welcome you to hatred of political chicanery and corruption by which men selected as public servants become betrayers and exploiters of the public welfare instead of its guardians and protectors, and thus hasten the day of fascism in America and the defeat of democracy. We welcome you to the hatred of all those forces and agencies in our common life which make for militaristic warfare and foster the suicide of society.

We welcome you to combat, to a fellowship of unremitting effort for the overthrow of the common enemies, a fellowship of those who refuse to run away to places of safety, physical, psychological, educational, or ecclesiastical, but who, by courageous truth-telling, by aggressive organization of the forces of decency and good order through every brave leader and worthy agency, work for the quickening of men of good will to fight the public enemies.

To the fellowship of hatred and combat in the name of the Kingdom of God we welcome you. In the name of all the long succession of prophets and fighters for social justice, going back to the Hebrew prophets and to Him who drove the money changers out of the temple, who flayed hypocrisy and greed and savage power. We welcome you, Al, to your full share of high hatred and combat, to your full share in the achievement of the Kingdom.

We welcome you, secondly, to a fellowship of love and gentleness and human sharing. We are ever thankful that in the midst of evil systems, forces, and powers there are always people to love and to treat with gentleness and human sharing. First, of course, are those who are in the inner circles of our families and friends. But way out beyond these the circles widen to include all men, women, and children who are sick and needy, dispossessed and unemployed, exploited and forsaken. Even beyond these are included those who are themselves exploiters and the savage strong who sin against us all and often know it not. Even these are within the compassion of Divine Love and so must be within the circle of our own, however much we hate the things they do, the forces they wield, the systems for which they stand.

And so we welcome you to a fellowship of universal love—forgiving and redeeming love—a fellowship of gentleness and human sharing. I have recently been informed by a young graduate of one of our theological seminaries that the ethic of love is not to be trusted any more as the chief agency of the Kingdom of God. "It doesn't win the battle," he says, "it lacks finality." He may be right, but I doubt it! He cannot name me the power that is more compelling. And so we welcome you to the fellowship of those who in love and humble service care for the sick, the ignorant, and the suffering, who sense the beauty and the sacredness of little children, of motherhood and fatherhood, who would conserve by personal ministry the sacred circle of the family, the Christian home, and who want to make such a home and family possible for all men and women.

We welcome you, therefore, on behalf of all the priests of human life, pastors and teachers, doctors, nurses, and Red Cross workers, friends and neighbors, parents, grandparents, and maiden aunts, older sisters, brothers, monks and nuns, rabbis and priests, and all the missionaries of the cross who serve in lonely outposts in the mountains or in lumber camps or crowded slums—all who in love and human sharing give in themselves their own interpretations of Eternal Love.

MINISTER AS INTERPRETER OF ETERNAL VALUES

We welcome you to a fellowship which works without hope of prestige or gain and without thought of worldly reward. With ever heightening intelligence of method, with ever deepening and widening of love may you reach out to the ministry of every human life you have a chance to touch. Here's to your love of your own child, Al, and all that she and her mother shall come to symbolize to you of the far-flung human need for love and gentleness in the whole wide family of God.

We welcome you next to a fellowship of open-mindedness and search for truth. No one who has watched for a quarter of a century and more the unbelievable discoveries in knowledge about our human life and expanded his horizons with the expansions of truth, can rest content with the conceptions of yesterday. Along with overt evil will and ruthless selfishness, ignorance and mental lethargy are to be seen as arch-enemies of the Kingdom.

We welcome you to a fellowship which refuses to run on dead issues or superseded knowledge and the conceptions of yesterday. This is in a peculiar sense true of our Congregational ministry. Our New England forefathers knew what they were about when they insisted on an educated ministry. Though we have in great areas of our thinking outgrown their conceptions, they would be the first to rejoice thereat. We welcome you to a fellowship one of whose priceless traditions is freedom from the slavish following of any tradition, from merely running in old grooves, merely following precedents. There is no substitute in this fellowship for the constant application of constructive critical intelligence to all the problems of human life and welfare. With all lovers of truth we follow hard after truth and welcome it from every quarter. We welcome it upon every aspect of human life, even upon the sacred values of religion, even the truth about ourselves, however distasteful. Never forgetting the values in old truths, we welcome every new truth that aids in the warfare against the enemies of society and empowers us for effective ministry to human need. In the name of all searchers for truth, all scholars and teachers, scientists and researchers who seek with unremitting labor the truth that maketh free, and also in the name of all wise counselors and interpreters who bring truth home to human hearts, we welcome you. We receive you to the guild of life-long students and questers after truth.

If I were to put it in a word, Al, I would dare to hazard the belief that, however high and wide and deep your search shall go, you will not surpass the boundaries of the truth that is in Jesus Christ our Lord, who understood indeed that which is in man and needed not that any modern sophisticate should tell Him its deep essential meanings.

And finally we welcome you to a fellowship of trust in God and to spiritual discipline. We shall not have come very far on the road toward social reconstruction without encountering forces beyond our control, not very far in the effort to heal the hurt of human life without awareness of the enormity of human need, nor very far in the search for truth without discovering that the known is to the unknown as a drop of water to the oceans vastness. We are all the time thrown back on God, on ultimate power and goodness and truth, on ultimate cosmic processes and forces. There is ultimate power that works for justice and love and truth in human affairs. Our weakness stands over against His strength, our meagerness over against His almighty resources, our disloyalty over against His loyalty, our petty selfishness over against His universal love. As we grow into spiritual maturity, into a fellowship of trust and faith and hope, we finally learn to say to Jesus, "Great Revealer, we believe in Thee, and thereby we believe in ultimate Goodness, Truth, and Love." We hazard our lives upon this great faith. We accept the spiritual disciplines of life. If dark frustrations come, if defeat and disappointments come, we shall accept the fellowship of His suffering and rejoice therein. We see beyond the present, for we are born of a faith that overleaps time and heartache, all present brutalities and the apparent victories of evil. Afar off we see the city of God, the towers whereof reach into heaven itself.

In the name of all fighters for justice, lovers in all the ages, searchers for truth wherever truth may lead, and the faith-filled who have put their trust in Him and accepted the spiritual disciplines of life—in the name of all these, the latchet of whose shoes we are not worthy to unloose, we welcome you and give you the right hand of fellowship to the Christian ministry.[16]

THE PERSON-MINDED MINISTRY AN INCARNATION

It is apparent, then, that the final test of interpretation in the ministry is the test of quality. Deeper than what he believes or does or says, or how he does it or states it, must be the life-bringing quality of the man himself. He is to be the incarnation of his message. This is where erring men such as we are draw back, as did Moses long ago when the Lord summoned him saying to him, in spite of all his declinations, "Thou shalt be unto him *as God*." Humbling as that terrific testing of the quality of his life may be, it is exalting too, exalting and demanding. How can he ever match his life to that ideal? Yet that ideal will swing his life up out of the tawdry and the commonplace, inward and outward, deep down, high up, and then onward. "As God"—as a "wonderful counselor," as a quickener and guide of voluntary groups, as a creative partner in the realm of love that is yet to be, as an interpreter of Eternal Love. What a calling!

"Jehovah complex?" Just the reverse! "I am among you as he that serveth." The whole of him, his every deed, word, and thought are to be dedicated to Eternal Love.

Thoughts hardly to be packed
Into a narrow act,
Fancies that broke through language and escaped;
All I could never be,
All, men ignored in me,
This, I was worth to God, whose wheel the pitcher shaped.[17]

---

[16] "The Right Hand of Fellowship," by the Reverend Richard H. Edwards, to the Reverend Alva Tompkins at his ordination, November 29, 1935, at the New England Congregational Church, Chicago, Illinois.

[17] Robert Browning, "Rabbi Ben Ezra."

A PERSON-MINDED MINISTRY

He is a freely creating "I Am," not living or working alone, but surrounded by the vast fellowship of aspiring men and women who say "we love," "we share," both he and they supported, suffused, and encompassed by the great "I Am," in whom they live and move and have their being.

X

PREPARATION FOR A PERSON-MINDED MINISTRY [1]

A POINT OF VIEW

THE topic is "Preparation for a Person-Minded Ministry"—stated thus—rather than "Theological Education." The differing connotations of these contrasted phrases may be suggestive, but the central theme, whatever the caption, is the preparation of young men and women for the Christian ministry. I interpret the ministry as always a ministry to persons, to persons in society, and preparation for it as training for a great profession.

When I think of the simple beauty, the inherent dignity of the word ministry, its breadth and richness, the heritage of human sharing carried by it, I do not think of the ordained ministry alone nor chiefly. I think of friends and neighbors in times of illness and distress, of nurses and Red Cross workers, of those who care for dependent and neglected children, of all those who serve in hospitals, of doctors on their endless rounds, of surgeons with their great responsibilities, of the teachers of youth in schools and colleges, and of missionaries on the wide fronts of Christendom. I think, indeed, in the mood of Jesus, of all servants and caretakers at their routine jobs, of fishermen, farmers, and all food producers, of

[1] This chapter is the author's earliest statement of the thesis contained in this book. It was read and discussed at a meeting of faculty members and students of Drew Theological Seminary on March 21, 1934, at the invitation of President Arlo Brown. The original form has been retained except that a section with regard to persons and one with regard to the social emphasis have been incorporated in earlier chapters.

carpenters and all tradesmen who minister to the necessities of men, and of the miners laboring deep underground. Most of all I think of mothers and fathers. They bear incalculably the greatest load of ministry to human lives, to say nothing of grandmothers, older brothers, sisters, and maiden aunts.

Upon this massive background of unordained human ministry by persons to persons, I see our professional ministry as a relatively meager group, a bit awkward and cumbersome, lacking facile skills in dealing with people, for the most part tragically unprepared and ill-prepared for their superlative functions in relation to human life.

The word "minded" in our topic connotes far more than a focus of thought upon persons, more than concern for them. It suggests a ministry that utilizes all the resources of scientific knowledge about persons, every bit of knowledge which is available right up to the running edge of new discovery. In no other field of research is there a more challenging body of new knowledge than that with regard to personality and social relationships. Surely we have no right in preparing for a ministry to persons to content ourselves with superseded knowledge or unwarranted assumptions about them; neither have we a right to proceed upon the basis of ignorance or false beliefs with regard to them. We have no right to speak about "man" merely as an abstraction, a sort of logical counterpart of God. Such a conception has been drained dry of all the concrete realities that characterize the multiplex lives of persons.

PREPARATION

Protestant ministers lack suitable preparation. A "minded" approach to persons in the fullest sense of the word includes both knowledge of human nature and of human needs and of how these needs have been and can be met. The tragic paucity of such knowledge among ministers is exposed in the most challenging single fact revealed in Mark May's report upon our noble profession. The fact is that less than half of the Protestant white ministers in America have had college training, whatever that may mean; and if all Protestant ministers, colored as well as white, are counted only one in five has had that much education. This indicates that certain large denominational groups have in effect no educational requirements for their ministers. No other great profession has allowed itself to be caught in the shifting sands of ignorance to such a degree as ours. Four-fifths of us have to educate ourselves as best we can. Such a fact makes it highly important for all of us to be clear about the essentials of preparation. Our New England forefathers knew what they were about when they insisted on an educated ministry. They moved in a historic tradition of professional leadership; but the demands of millions of people who required religious ministry, as the national life extended westward, soon outran the supply of trained men. We would not overlook the indispensable services of ministers who have never been through college or seminary, but who have persistently educated themselves. Yet the inadequacy of training on the part of many men, especially those who serve the poorer white and negro churches constitutes nothing less than a national tragedy. They represent the quantitative as well as the qualitative lack of preparation.

Some of the rest of us are ill-prepared because we have been so largely the victims of a theory and system of education which has lacked the organizing center in persons here suggested. One is forced, for instance, to recognize the perversions of ministry that have been set going in the name of scholarship, to say nothing of much worse perversions due to ignorance or to fixed ideas about irrelevant details or distorted beliefs. Here are perversions due to bloodless philosophical abstractions made on the ancient fallacy that the real discloses itself in abstract verbalizations more clearly than in concrete personal experience, in endless emphases upon various theories of the Godhead and abstruse lectures upon lifeless doctrines derived therefrom. Think of the volumes of fine-spun technicalities piled up in seminary libraries, without a trace of relationship to human needs, volumes of analytical studies that never arrive at any synthesized meanings. On their shelves also are accumulations of detached facts which have no pertinence to everyday living. Specialization has been given to researches in historical matters quite unrelated to the cure of souls or society, to investigations into biblical details involving no possible living issue, to linguistic requirements out of all consonance with any modern possibility of use in an active ministry. Such errors of emphasis have been chiefly due to the absence of a dominating interest in persons, in the living issues of life. Subject-centered professors trained in the German method have too often superimposed upon their students research problems personally interesting to themselves as technical scholars, but with little if any reference to the goal of a direct ministry to people. In contrast a goal related to living persons implies courses in the disciplines essential to a truly functional ministry, and that in modern life as it is. Such a goal calls for seminary students to become ministers rather than technical scholars. Those who teach in divinity schools are no more liberated from the criterion of the usability of the knowledge which they select for emphasis than are those who guide social workers, nurses, physicians, or surgeons.

If it is an effective ministry to persons for which these young men and women are to be prepared, then important issues are involved in the selection of teaching materials and in emphases to be made in the courses taught. There will be visible contrasts between courses chosen on such a basis and those which primarily feature research for the Ph.D. degree. The latter properly belong in a half-dozen departments of a university graduate school and are in their places of scholarly value. The failure to accept the full implications of the ministry as a person-minded rather than a subject-minded affair has been the cause of many distortions of emphasis even in the better seminaries. It has left many seminary graduates ill-prepared to cope with the living issues in the lives of persons.

General preparation. Preparation for the ministry must of course begin long before students get to the seminary. We assume at once those preparations of motive and purpose, those habits of mind which accentuate clean unselfish living and thinking, freedom from personal exhibitionism, persistent human interest, deep convictions about Jesus, courageous faith in the dependability of the universe and in the possibility of a better social order. All the elementary courses leading to a sound culture must also be assumed. The pursuit of knowledge about persons demands a searching course in psychology, especially social psychology. This should follow at least one course in physiology, back of which should have been a course in general biology. There ought also to have been adequate introductory courses in sociology, in general literature, including the Bible, together with much continued personal reading in these fields. Stress should be laid also upon the great biographies, the great fiction, the great dramas, and all the enduring literature which carries forward the spiritual interpretation of persons in relationships as well as the best traditions of our common culture. We must also assume, before entrance to the seminary, broad general courses in economics, history, and philosophy, also courses in general science orientating the student in modern scientific knowledge about the nature of the world and of man. In these courses there should have developed in each student an initial grasp of the scientific method and a realization of the importance of objectivity toward all bodies of data, including the religious.

There should have been fostered the ability to build hypotheses and test them by facts, and to classify facts upon which to erect hypotheses, as well as the ability to offer constructive criticism of the methods and results of others.

Such preparation cannot always be assumed before seminary entrance, nor should those who do not have it always be denied admission on the basis of arbitrary standards. Such a lack on the part of some able applicants intensifies the argument for the greater individualization of seminary training, for orientation courses based on the discovered needs of students, and for skillful personal counseling with students, especially at entrance and during the first seminary year. All this could be done without lowering of standards.

Special studies of people in life situations. Upon our thesis the seminary course should early include intensive studies of people in typical human situations and relationships. It should never lose sight of normal happy living—regenerate, beautiful living—both as a goal and as a present fact in the lives of many men and women in families and in other groups. But the basic assumption concerning the minister is that he is to help people do something about their lives whenever he discovers illness or wrongness of any kind which needs healing. His approach is normative. He aims at adjustments on the highest possible levels. He needs a fundamental basis of knowledge, therefore, about the stresses and strains in people's lives. The tension points in ordinary living ought to have his early attention. Such points of strain, when unrelieved, develop into pathological states affecting ever wider areas in the life and lead to flabby weaknesses, evil habits, and broken relationships. They finally lead on the individual side to personal demoralization. They lead on the social side to ruptures and disorganization in society. It is a matter of great significance to ministers that the modern study of social pathology includes these two bodies of data.

PREPARATION FOR A PERSON-MINDED MINISTRY

Social pathology is precisely a study of personal demoralization and social disorganization. These two bodies of facts about which the minister is to do something must, of course, be known before the minister can know what he is to do. Social pathology with its twofold interest, personal and social, stands at the very starting point, therefore, of direct preparation for a ministry to persons in situations. Let us be clear at once, however, that we do not mean a preponderant study of the abnormal. There is danger, indeed, that abnormal psychology may become for seminary students merely an outlet for prurient curiosity. Students need first to ask what are the modern life-breakers for ordinary men and women, what are the facts of personal frustration and shattering, of social misunderstanding, of social bitterness and rupture. These facts are indispensable for the minister to know before he seriously attempts to do anything about these facts. Let us be wholly candid at this point. Neither he nor his professors can any longer assume that he already knows them. It is a stiff and continuing task to catch up with these facts and keep up on them in the midst of modern sociological and psychological discoveries. And next, beyond the facts themselves and something of their human meanings he must know what the agencies and services are by which effective ministries to these needs are already being supplied. At a minimum this work in social pathology would include a year-long intensive course, incorporating a careful survey at least of remedial measures.

Such a general course needs to be paralleled and enriched by firsthand studies of groups of persons in whom the student already has some genuine personal interest. In my own intermittent seminary teaching I have found no more rewarding project than to ask each student to specialize upon the strains involved in the life issues of some particular group of people personally known to him. Such "case groups," as we have called them, have included the following and many others: unemployed boys ages sixteen to twenty in urban surroundings, young engaged and married couples eighteen to thirty, farm men and women over fifty, unskilled Italian laborers forty to fifty, middle-aged women widowed or otherwise detached from men, high-school boys and girls thirteen to eighteen, "shut-ins" among older men and women, physically handicapped boys twelve to eighteen, dependent men and women mostly aged in a county home, a selected group of "trouble-making" women of all ages, patients in a tuberculosis hospital. These are but a few of some sixty selected case groups chosen in a course which included older men in the active ministry as well as seminary students. All of these cases were elected on the basis of personal interest.

Studies of such case groups have given the students who worked upon them deeper insights into actual stresses and strains among members of such groups, and into some of the causal factors of difficulty involved in their experiences. Knowledge of successful adjustments being made by some of the persons in these groups was also secured. These studies have given fresh views, as by spotlight and microscope, upon bits of the actual tissue of modern life, its tensions, its breaking points, and some of its stronger holding fibers. A student's early philosophy of life gets a genuine testing in this way, and his questions become living questions rather than academic ones. This is merely one aspect of method for preliminary studies of living people in actual situations. But it provides a challenging experience to students whose training in other courses is chiefly in history, theology, biblical literature, and kindred subjects. In many seminary students the power of direct social observation has not been trained, and their experience outside their own social strata has been very limited. Such studies need to be supplemented by carefully guided field work.

By these means there can be established early in the seminary course a much richer knowledge of actual people set in the texture of modern life than is now provided for in most seminaries. As a matter of fact, the first year in many seminaries moves in exactly the opposite direction, away from concrete first-hand human factors to studies of a technical nature. A minister will, of course, need many years of personal contacts in active service to enrich his knowledge of the human story to full depth and breadth. Without direct study of people during the seminary years, however, such knowledge might never be really established at all. Without it he might easily drift on in bookish detachment, as so many ministers have done, with permanently implanted academic attitudes, with behavior patterns of avoidance and escape. He would thus be bereft of first-hand knowledge of the issues of life, be without informed ability to grapple with those issues on his own or any other person's behalf. With person-mindedness actively cultivated, however, a solid groundwork can be laid during the first seminary year for an effective ministry to persons and to groups. By these approaches students are in position, with their feet on the ground, to move from case group situations intimately known to others less familiar, and on through local community problems out to the broader issues of a Christian social order. This is the sequence by which they can ordinarily come most effectively to the realization of the manifold tasks to be undertaken in a ministry to individuals, to groups, and to society.

Studies in what Christianity contributes to modern persons. With the study and understanding of human needs thus considered we are ready for a second main emphasis, which is much better established in the seminary curriculum than that just described. This emphasis comes in answer to the questions: What distinctive meanings have the life and teaching of Jesus in relation to these human needs? What are the distinctive Christian insights and emphases which now have pertinence and value for the rectification of human life? These questions must of course be answered in the light of Hebrew life and thought and of Christian history, as well as by open-minded comparison of Christianity with the teachings and practices of other religious faiths. The answers to these questions must have backgrounds in a philosophy of history and of religion and of the function of religion in social change. They must carry forward the spiritual traditions of a vital faith. They must include disciplines in the biblical literature, in systematic thinking about the Christian concept of God and Christian ethics in human relationships. The whole aspect of preparation which attempts to interpret essential Christianity in its historic setting is already so well provided in all the better schools that deep appreciation is our mood in regard to it and full recognition of its rightful place as bulking large in seminary studies. There has recently come, however, a wholesome sharpening of inquiry as to the relevance of such knowledge for modern life. Our age wants to know not only what the teaching is in itself and in its original setting, but also what it means for present persons and society. Quite specifically it asks how Jesus and His teachings make a difference with us modern men in modern situations and what that difference is. This incisive demand from all kinds of modern realists has been burning up a lot of chaff—great masses of verbiage which have long overlaid and obscured the central human meanings of the teachings of Jesus. Now the distinctive messages of Christianity stand clearly forth.

Preparation for the ministry as an art. The argument moves from this point to a special emphasis in preparation. We now in a sense move out of the realm of the sciences into the realm of art. We move on to the creative art of Christian ministry. Every great art rests directly upon certain sciences, upon knowledge of the facts with which that art has most to do, the facts most germane to it. What we have been suggesting thus far is the necessity of a basis of knowledge of human experience and of essential Christianity upon which the art of the Christian ministry can be erected. How about the art itself? Strictly speaking, an art cannot be taught. It has to be achieved by the artist himself by the use of insights, skills, and techniques playing upon the materials most pertinently available to his art—be it portraiture, sculpture, music, or the art of ministry. On the other hand, it is clear that insights can be quickened by a great teacher, skills developed, techniques acquired. These can all be fused into high achievement by the artist himself working intelligently under guidance to develop his own artistic powers.

For pastoral counseling. Two main lines of further study open at this point. The first of these is the art of personal counseling. Call it, if you prefer, the spiritual culture of individuals, the pastoral ministry, or the cure of souls. It necessitates an ever-deepening knowledge of persons, preferably of individual persons in some case group that one has studied. Still deeper insights into personal experience must be achieved, still deeper knowledge of persons in intimate situations, deeper knowledge of the hidden inner meanings of their lives. An intensive study of personal records is necessary. One has to ask wherein have counselors in particular situations succeeded and wherein have they failed. It is necessary to study instances of physical handicap, of maladjustment in personal social relations, of moral and spiritual confusion, of pre-marital and marital difficulties, of tensions between parents and children, of vocational maladjustments, and of mental illness in varying degrees of intensity. The biographies of great persons and the fiction which portrays great characters are essential, as well as the more recent psychological books in this field.

Such a course also necessitates a study of methods in counseling and utilizes a knowledge of the best types of personal and social work techniques—how to secure contacts, how to establish rapport, how to secure the more accessible objective data, and how to get at the more elusive inner data, the fears, prejudices, loyalties, and motivations which influence the person. He who would counsel must understand what is involved in the art of a shared inquiry—a mutual diagnosis—in the realization and the acceptance of the meanings of all the facts as mutually discovered. He must know what is required in the rectification of motives, attitudes, and relationships, in re-education, in rethinking the main purpose and program of the life, and in a long-time follow-up relationship. For the Christian minister it is essential above all to understand the actual available resource power which Jesus, in His person, His message, and His methods, may supply to the counselor and counselee alike. This is very far from suggesting that the pastor should become an amateur psychoanalyst; but it is to suggest that he must be a capable and qualified general counselor, must know when and where he can and ought to counsel and when and where he ought to call in the specialists, and must be prepared to do both effectively.

Through such a study, brought deeply into a student's consciousness by actual work of his own with individuals, he can be guided in the development of his own life-long ministry to persons in their life situations, in families, and in other group relationships. Surely we all agree on the personal pastoral ministry as a primary and permanent aspect of our professional service. Yet we have to remember how relatively ineffective pastoral calling has, for the most part, been, and how urgent is the need for a new development of this type of ministry under seminary leadership. Does anything else have right to precedence?

For social action. Let us turn to the more social side. A student who deals honestly and thoroughly with individuals will get first-hand knowledge of their personal situations and the social groupings in which they are. First-hand knowledge of such situations supplies the true basis for the study of social needs and social problems. First-hand studies of life experiences will take him directly into a deeper understanding of the broader problems in the life of the community, the nation, and the world. By reason of that deeper understanding a student will be well nigh forced to grow into the Christian social ministry.

Think of Walter Rauschenbusch grappling at first hand with the actual problems of congested living in lower New York. Out of his experience came *Christianity and the Social Crisis*. Think of Harry Ward immersed in living issues in people's lives around about the stockyards of Chicago before he created the Methodist Federation for Social Service, wrote his books, and went on to his later teaching. Think how Albert Schweitzer, determined that life should not rob him of first-hand experience, plunged into the tragic illnesses of the African west coast, a prerequisite to his world service. Think of Kagawa in that impossible little hut in the slums of Kobe welcoming gamblers, murderers, and prostitutes, learning from them as he tried to teach them the essentials of the Christian answer to human need. This was his preparation for the Kingdom of God Movement throughout Japan and for a world-wide ministry.

It is precisely because so many students in the seminaries are jumping over these first essential steps in experience and are arriving (sometimes under doctrinaire professors) at doctrinaire opinions about capitalism, socialism, communism, non-resistance, the use of force, and other factors affecting social change, that they find themselves quite up in the air. Theoretical conflicts about the Christian answers to the problems of society are inevitable in such a seminary situation. This is the main reason why the priceless actual answers of Christianity are so often ignored or falsely identified with some particular line of social theory or particular type of economic or social reform. We have yet to learn that first-hand experience is indispensable in any deep process of education whatsoever. We have yet to learn that most actual social solutions are multiple solutions. We have yet to learn that the Christian message is too widely inclusive a message to be confined to any single proposal. The incalculable values in it cannot be realized by intellection apart from social experience and social action. There is no quick or simple way. There is no short cut to the new society. One visualizes nevertheless a thoroughgoing laboratory course in Christian social thinking and a long-sustained, free, yet skillfully guided period of experimentation in a whole series of specific situations—personal, group, local community, regional, national, and world.

Let any seminary student who really wants to find social solutions instead of mere emotional relief search for the Christian answers to social injustices now breaking the lives of people he personally knows in his own native region. Such near ends of national social problems will give him leading strings to the wider maladjustments which he is to help solve. Let him give first-hand attention to neglected children, poverty-stricken homes, political inefficiency and graft, sterile education in the schools, depressed groups of unemployed, scorned racial groups, the groups branded as criminals. Let him study the influence and methods of some small oligarchy of powerful businessmen or World War legionaires who would suppress freedom of speech and try to keep a strangle hold on community leaders, including ministers, who might be shapers of public opinion. Or let him, for example, know the actual life experiences of farm men and women in his own countryside. That will take him into the wider sweep of the national and world agricultural problem with all its ramifications and exploitations. As he works at these he will learn of many agencies which are also working in this field, or perhaps he will learn of the lack of such agencies. He will inevitably be challenged by the need for ministers who are quickeners of community conscience. Similarly with first-hand knowledge of other groups he may arrive with some social intelligence at his own ministry to persons in society. This is the ministry supremely worth his while.

In the social ministry many able younger men are now questioning and experimenting realistically as to social methods. Agree or disagree with them as one may, they are asking the seminaries for skillful guidance in that experimentation. They are convinced searchers and experimenters rather than "red radicals." They are asking what new methods of social action are really needed to supplement those already tested and established. They need from the seminaries guidance in their search for answers to such questions as these: What methods actually effect social change beneficially? Which are truly in the mood of Jesus? Which are not? How much, by any objective social test, do we accomplish with such benevolences as Christmas baskets? How about our support of family welfare work, our support of institutions for dependent and neglected children? What does Sunday morning preaching on social issues actually accomplish? How wide and deep does it go? How about forums and group discussions on social issues for those outside the church as well as in it? How about discussions with groups of negroes or other racial minority groups, or joint services of worship with them? How about a minister's sharing in investigations of racial, industrial, and political maladjustments? How about risking arrest and imprisonment in the cause of free speech? How about a minister's taking sides in industrial conflicts? How about opposing military propaganda, or telling the truth to political bosses and demigogues face to face, or to dangerous crowds inflamed by passion and prejudice?

Which, if any, and *if any, which* of these methods are effective in the social expansion of a Christian order of society? Which are subversive of it? Every one of these methods and many others are being tried out, wisely or unwisely, by active ministers somewhere in America today; yet few seminaries are providing any systematic consideration of the relative usefulness of such methods, of their Christian or un-Christian character. What right have the seminaries to lag behind in helping students to clarify their thinking and action as to such methods? Social conservatives and social radicals alike need fair-minded, systematic consideration of these issues.

In methods. The stereotyped methods of the churches and of seminary training are up for review in other ways. Many intelligent laymen are asking, for example: Why the continuance of such a disproportionate emphasis upon preaching as a method of spreading the messages of Jesus, as if the entire life of the church depended on it alone? They ask this without the slightest failure to recognize a true and indispensible function for preaching. But why is there a continued insensitiveness to the widespread waning of popular response to hortatory forms of address? Why is there a relative underemphasis upon other functions of the ministry, such as the organization of intimate interest groups within the church on lines of age, family status, spiritual affinity, or community goals? How about genuinely effective leadership in the religious education of the young? How about taking seriously the possibilities of adult education on questions having to do with vital problems, as, for example, the rearing of children and more effective public education? How about training in better methods of leading group discussions, or any one of many other methods of achieving spiritual results? Many of these methods are now ignored or little stressed in many seminaries. If one were to throw this whole query into the terms of medical preparation, one would inquire if the seminaries are not short on the equivalents of physiology, anatomy, and pathology—long on materia medica, but very short on all the techniques of practice except preaching?

Is it not obvious that the arts required in a person-minded ministry now call for fuller cultivation?

SOME POSSIBLE ADJUSTMENTS IN THE SEMINARIES

We therefore take further thought about possible adjustments in the seminaries. Some changes have been made in recent years from former static and rigid requirements. Many of these adjustments have been made, however, merely by adding new elective courses and regrouping old courses—much as curriculum adjustments were attempted in the public schools by addition of more subjects. Frankly, this does not achieve the result we seek. A fundamental reorganization of courses around a functional center in persons, the values that inhere in persons, their potential power as Christian persons to change society, is essential. Such an orientation of viewpoint is suggested as that, for example, which is shown in the twelfth edition of the *Encyclopedia Britannica,* which is written, in contrast to former editions, from the viewpoint of the reader instead of from the viewpoint of the technical scholarly writer. If the ministry is to be thought of as a purposive art of service to persons in modern relationships, the issue cannot be evaded nor met by compromises or half measures. If we are dealing on the one hand with a subject-centered curriculum the end of which is erudition and a learned scholarly ministry in the old sense of the word, with ministers living in a static world, their citizenship in heaven or among other intelligentsia, that is one thing. If, on the other hand, we are dealing with a creative task which can be satisfied with nothing less than the art of effective ministry to all people in the multiple situations and demands of modern life, that is quite another thing, and the issue clears.

If our central thesis be accepted, curriculum provisions will adjust themselves. They must. Much that is now in the curriculum will be seen to have permanent place as essential resource material for the minister's work, but much that has been dealt with in the more technical courses in all departments will either be humanized for the use of person-minded ministers or go out to its proper place in a university graduate school. No detailed suggestions on course adjustments is possible here, in addition to those already made, but surely the great essential messages of the Old and New Testaments which constitute the enduring biblical values should continue to have a central place as resource materials. It goes without saying that the history of the Christian Church and Christian thought and Christian social action through the centuries should continue to have large emphasis, but with constant concern for present needs and future possibilities. Such courses will take into account the issue of pertinence and will deal more fully with the history of efforts toward spiritual healing and toward the future achievement of a more Christian order of society.

A word about adjustments in preparation for specific ministerial functions. The death of thousands of little independent churches in recent years is a sign of profound change, on the whole a sign of progress. As independent units many of them ought to die, for we have clearly come to the end of the era which they represented with their excessive localism, cantankerous divisiveness, and off-center emphases. On the other hand, the staff ministries which are now being slowly developed in the so-called "larger parishes" in agricultural areas, as well as in metropolitan churches, mark the new day in the unification process. Still an ideal, rather than a widespread fact, they are significant nevertheless. This is not solely because a wider neighborhood can now be covered by modern transportation and telephones, but also because a staff ministry makes possible a group fellowship, team play, and better salaries. Important also is the specialization of function made possible. Some degree of specialization brings out the varying abilities of ministers and releases them from the jack-of-all-trades set-up under which they have been compelled to serve. A staff ministry covering a unified countryside, when it is thoroughly worked out, gives all the men and women members of it a chance to do the particular work for which they are especially qualified and for which they will someday be even more specifically prepared.

The unified countryside necessary to a fully successful larger parish must be scientifically determined in each instance. Such an area should be a unit from the point of view of geography, a valley with surrounding hill country, or the like; of economics, buying, selling, and shipping points; of education, centralized school or group of school districts; and of social life with population socially homogeneous. The particular specializations in function in any given staff ministry will depend upon the individual abilities of those who compose it. An illustrative combination would be: (1) the preacher-organizer doing some pastoral service; (2) the pastor-case-worker doing some speaking; (3) the educational, recreational, social group leader. Other specializations will need to be developed in drama, music, and business management. The leadership of community causes and movements must also be borne in mind. Larger opportunities for women in such a staff ministry, according to their special gifts, become available. During the depression all specialization of functions has been largely in abeyance, but the issue is already coming to the fore in many regions in relation to inevitable consolidations into larger parishes.

A wider variety of types of ability might be utilized and trained in the ministry if functional specialization were developed. In every seminary there are students who are eager for counsel in discovering their own best forms of service in the ministry—specialized forms perhaps. They want mature guidance faithfully sustained by a competent faculty counselor. Field work both during and following the seminary years can be made a true basis for such continuous counseling and heightened efficiency in service.

HOW PREPARE TO COMMUNICATE THE SENSE OF THE PRESENCE OF GOD?

Finally, we come to the most delicate of all aspects of preparation—how to learn to communicate to others the sense of the presence of God. Frankly, I do not know how it is learned or taught, save as one lives daily in the sense of that Great Presence through the whole sweep of preparation for the ministry, as well as in deep experience with the life problems of men and women. Sometimes I am sure no man can teach other men how to communicate it save by doing it unconsciously himself if and when the presence of God is a living reality to him. At any rate, we all talk too much about it and achieve it far too little. We are all grateful, of course, to those seminary professors who are able to help their students escape from personal idiosyncrasies and infelicities in their efforts to conduct public worship, especially so if they are genuinely interested in them individually and get down to the deeper issues in their lives, to any personal maladjustments that may be there. We are grateful to teachers who communicate a realization of the dignity of worship, who emphasize worthy forms of liturgy, and music that is consonant with a great and beautiful experience. But I confess to a sense of labored effort, a sort of pedestrian inadequacy in most services of worship. Yet I have little to suggest that is not already being done. Perhaps it is because, for some of us, the sense of the Eternal breaks through when and where it will, whenever the soul is ready. The inner light shineth when it listeth. It is not always between eleven and twelve o'clock on a Sunday morning. At any rate, the ability to reveal something of the resources of the Everlasting God to other persons must arise in one's own soul out of absolutely honest experience. The sense of the Eternal must be caught as it flashes through the veil in moments of meditation, in hours of suffering, in moments of exaltation, in times of great responsibility. Sometimes it comes in utter solitude when one is on a lonely country road, sometimes on a hilltop, or by the ocean shore at sunset silent with a friend, when

> It is beauteous evening, calm and free,
>   The holy time is quiet as a Nun
>   Breathless with adoration; the broad sun
> Is sinking down in its tranquility;
> The gentleness of heaven broods o'er the Sea;
>   Listen! The mighty Being is awake
>   And doth with his eternal motion make
> A sound like thunder—everlastingly.[2]

Whenever and wherever one is moved to bare the head as in God's nearer presence, then is a time and there a place of native worship. It is a sublime experience, quite unarted. However, it seems to be necessary under the conditions of our life to regularize the times of worship indoors, and we must all be grateful that there are those who by reason of inner exaltation of spirit, well sustained, can induce a genuine worship experience more or less regardless of time and setting. There are, God be thanked, still some ministers who, like the great poets, have the gifts of insight and expression joined. The rest of us never achieve their power to know or communicate the full sense of the presence of the Eternal; but we rejoice in them, the great religious mystics. We may not reach the

[2] William Wordsworth, "It is a Beauteous Evening."

authentic clarity of their insights; but we can at least bow in reverent gratitude with them, learn from them, and give to our people the very best we have. Here is a true revelation of the soul of one of them:

> Oft when the Word is on me to deliver
>   Lifts the illusion and the truth lies bare;
> Desert or throng, the city or the river,
>   Melts in a lucid Paradise of air,—
>
> Only like souls I see the folk thereunder,
>   Bound who should conquer, slaves who should be kings,—
> Hearing their one hope with an empty wonder,
>   Sadly contented in a show of things;—
>
> Then with a rush the intolerable craving
>   Shivers throughout me like a trumpet-call,—
> Oh to save these! to perish for their saving,
>   Die for their life, be offered for them all! [3]

A distinguished university professor recently announced that of all the absurd positions for a man to hold, that of the Christian mystic is the most absurd. Quite possibly so, but who, may we inquire, gave the statisticians the right to rule the mystics out of court? Some of us prefer to plead guilty and humbly wish that we were more guilty, ever wistful to see more deeply into the mysterious brightness.

> While they deem my Lord is dead
> My eyes are on His shining head. . . . .
>
> Poor Lazarus shall wait in vain,
>   And Bartimaeus still go blind;
> The healing hem shall ne'er again
>   Be touched by suffering humankind.

[3] Frederic W. H. Myers, "Saint Paul."

> Yet all the while I see them rest,
> The poor and outcast, on His breast. . . . .
> Yet all the while my Lord I meet
> In every London lane and street.[4]

May the Eternal keep alive in us the mystic sense of the beauty of persons and of the beauty of the Lord our God. These best prepare us for a person-minded ministry.

[4] Richard Le Gallienne, "The Second Crucifixion." By permission of Dodd, Mead & Co.